Glimpses of
collection of Scriptu
that provide the readers with encouragement by
directing their thoughts back to the God of the Bible
who is love. Both authors honestly share their lives
and hearts through their very personal times of
challenges and celebrations that deepened their
faith in Christ, which is their same hope for anyone
who reads these daily meditations. You will benefit
from and enjoy this collection of reflections written
by two gifted women who love the God of love.

—Mark E. Shaw, D.Min.
  President of Truth in Love Ministries
  Author of *The Heart of Addiction* and 20 other
  books

Devotions are meant to point the reader to the
various characteristics of living a life devoted to
Almighty God. Shirley and Harriet do a spectacular
job of showing *Glimpses of the Savior* in the
everyday happenings we all encounter.

The "Prayers" were both meaningful and
beautiful. The "Thoughts for the Day" kept you
centered in the ultimate purpose of the devotional.
Glimpses of the Savior not only brings meaning and
purpose to the Thanksgiving, Christmas, and New
Year seasons but to every day of the year. I highly
recommend this book for reading any time of the
year!

—Mary L. Varga
  Author of *The Light Through My Tunnel:
  Overcoming Tragedy Through Courage and
  Faith*

Shirley and Harriet will capture your interest from the first page to the last with their unique connection to each other from childhood to their adult lives. Growing up together in Nigeria where their parents were missionaries, they have fascinating stories to tell throughout the book. You'll find glimpses of the Savior on each page to draw you closer to the Lord and enrich your spiritual life. And woven throughout the pages, humor is sprinkled so you smile often—and laugh, too. The 50 devotionals will draw you into discovering the many facets of prayer. The authors' testimonies of faith reveal their beautiful hearts and deep love for the Lord. You'll want to read this devotional from cover to cover immediately. I read it within a few weeks because I couldn't stop turning the pages. I plan to reread it during the holidays one devotion at a time to drink in the holiday messages so beautifully written with seasonal images portrayed through their words. A must read for your heart and soul for the holidays and all year long.

—Peggy Cunningham

Missionary and author of *Hooray for Holidays* children's series and *Shape Your Soul* devotional
www.PeggyCunningham.com

Glimpses of the Savior

Second Edition

Shirley Crowder
Harriet E. Michael
Illustrated by Kristin Michael

Shirley Crowder
Colossians 1:15-17

N

Glimpses of the Savior
Second Edition

© Copyright 2018 Shirley Crowder & Harriet E. Michael
Illustrated by: Kristin Michael

ISBN: **978-1-944120-63-4**

Published by:

Pix-N-Pens Publishing
PO Box 702852
Dallas, TX 75370
www.WriteIntegrity.com

Published in the United States of America.

Dedication

We dedicate this book to
MKs (missionary kids) everywhere and of all
ages,
who share our experience of holiday memories
on two continents,
and to
Jeannie Crowder,

Shirley's mom and Harriet's beloved
missionary aunt.
Jeannie made the MK experience wonderful
for two little girls who would someday
grow up and write books together.

Glimpses of the Savior

Preface

In early November, our minds turn to the upcoming holiday season. We get busy preparing for Thanksgiving, Christmas, and the New Year, and all too often, we forget the real meanings of these celebrations. As Christ-followers, we can guard against this by focusing our hearts on God's word.

Thanksgiving is a time to give God thanks; Christmas is the celebration of the birth of the Savior; the New Year brings new beginnings. This devotional contains fifty meditations to help you find Jesus among the celebrations and decorations. Begin using this devotional the first week of November, and it will carry you into the New Year and through mid-January.

We appreciate Lynette Bonner for designing our beautiful cover.

We are grateful for the encouragement and direction of our publisher and friend, Marji Laine Clubine, who worked tirelessly helping us publish this devotional.

Chapter 1: The Crispness of Fall

A Quiet Place

by Harriet
Read: Mark 6:30-32, Mark 1:35

Then, because so many people
were coming and going ...
he said to them, "Come with me by yourselves
to a quiet place and get some rest."
Mark 6:31 (NIV)

"I'm so busy, I don't know if I found a rope or lost my horse."

That's something I used to hear my grandfather say. Sadly, it is still true today. We are still busy beyond belief, aren't we? Our lives are filled with schedules, appointments, meetings, and more schedules. We have clocks, computers, calendars, cell phones, and other gadgets which beep and buzz at us all day long as they prod us on to our next appointment. We usually hurry out of the house in the morning and do not get back home until evening. When we finally do return home, sometimes quite late, there are e-mails to answer, dinners to cook, dishes to wash, and news to catch up on. If you have children, you can add supervising homework and putting in a load of laundry to that list too. Even at home we are, well, busy!

We are especially busy during the Thanksgiving, Christmas, and New Year seasons, are we not? These special days which should be enjoyed and savored are instead spent rushing through, trying to get everything done. There are gifts to buy and wrap, cards to send, decorations to put up, parties and family gatherings to attend, food to cook. And of course, we also have many special activities at church, like choir rehearsals and programs, children's pageants and activities, Sunday School functions, and on it goes! The list of things we feel we need to do during this time of year is seemingly endless.

Where does God fit into this fast-paced world of ours? My thoughts turn to the words of an old hymn, "Take Time to Be Holy." Written in 1882 by William Longstaff, it says,

> "Take time to be holy; speak oft
> with the Lord.
> Abide with Him always and
> feed on His Word …
> Take time to be holy;
> the world rushes on;
> Spend much time in secret
> with Jesus alone …
> Take time to be holy,

be calm in thy soul,
Each thought and each motive
beneath His control.
Thus led by His Spirit
to fountains of love,
Thou soon shalt be fitted
for service above."

In today's passage, we see times when Jesus sought solitude by spending time alone with His Father in prayer and worship. That is how we are able to be holy, or set apart, as 1 Peter 1:16 tells us to be. The hymn writer's exhortation to take time to be holy was not an original thought—he was simply encouraging us to follow Jesus' example.

But the concept goes back even before Jesus' time. In Isaiah 30:15 we read, "In repentance and rest is your salvation, in quietness and trust is your strength." Jesus invites us to come with Him to a quiet place. Will you and I take Him up on His invitation today? Let us remember the message of this hymn and the example Jesus gave and make it a priority during this holiday season, regardless of how busy our schedules may be.

Prayer: Heavenly Father, thank You for inviting us to spend time with You. Please help us in this fast-paced world in which we live. Help us keep up with all the demands on our time while also setting aside a quiet time to come away with You and rest. In Jesus' name, Amen.

Thought for the Day: Jesus invites us to spend time with Him. Let's make a practice of clearing our schedules as we make Him a priority in our lives this year.

For the Beauty of the Earth

by Shirley
Read: Psalm 148

Praise him, sun and moon,
praise him, all you shining stars!
Praise him, you highest heavens,
and you waters above the heavens!
Let them praise the name of the LORD!
For he commanded and they were created.
Psalm 148:3-6

After a long, hot, and humid summer, when I wake up to the first wave of fall's chilly crispness it is absolutely magnificent. It seems as if the entire universe has more energy, is full of vigor, excitement, and expectation. Just as quickly as the crisp air comes in, the beautiful colors of fall begin to emerge.

I love living in an area of the country that experiences four distinct seasons, and I am fascinated by trees in every stage and season. As chlorophyll is produced in the spring and summer, the leaves on the trees are green. As fall begins, some trees stop making chlorophyll, and the existing chlorophyll breaks down into smaller parts and disappears. When this happens, the other pigments whose colors are being overpowered by the chlorophyll's green can show their colors. The leaves on these trees begin turning from green to the resplendent fall colors of varying shades of red, yellow, purple, orange, and brown.

It is an awe-inspiring experience to see a mountainside full of trees with brilliantly covered leaves shining brightly in the sun as they wave in the cool breeze. I imagine the sound of the leaves rustling in the wind is the trees singing, and the leaves blowing in the wind is the trees clapping their hands as they praise their Creator (1 Chronicles 16:33; Isaiah 55:12).

Through creation we get glimpses of the majesty and glory of Creator God. The beauty of this season makes me sing "For the Beauty of the Earth", by Folliott S. Pierpoint. Its second verse and chorus are:

"For the wonder of each hour,
Of the day and of the night,
Hill and vale, and tree and flow'r,
Sun and moon, and stars and light—
Lord of all, to Thee we raise,
This our hymn of grateful praise."

The sunrises and sunsets this time of year are simply incredible and remind me of another hymn,

"The Heavens are Telling," by Joseph Haydn. It proclaims:

> "The heavens are telling
> the glory of God,
> The wonder of His work
> displays the firmament."

Romans 1:20 tells us that "his invisible attributes, namely, his eternal power and divine nature, have been clearly perceived, ever since the creation of the world, in the things that have been made." I've heard it said that creation was God's first missionary.

Creation also reminds us that God is omnipresent—everywhere at the same time. Isaac Watts wrote about this in the third verse of the hymn, "We Sing the Almighty Power of God":

> "There's not a plant or flower below
> but makes Your glories known,
> and clouds arise and tempests blow
> by order from Your throne;
> while all that borrows life from You
> is ever in your care,
> and everywhere that we can be,
> You, God, are present there."

Prayer: Thank You, Father, for the gift of this

beautiful world in which to live and minister. We thank You that we can see Your hand in the radiant colors of fall leaves and in stunning sunsets and wonders like the Grand Canyon. Open our eyes to see Your glory, majesty, power, and dominion in all of creation. In Jesus' name, Amen.

Thought for the Day: If the leaves on the trees and the stars praise God, along with the rest of His creation, we who are created in His image should praise Him all the more!

Apples of Gold

by Harriet
Read: James 3:6-8, Psalm 19:14

A word fitly spoken is like apples of gold
in pictures of silver.
Proverbs 25:11 (KJV)

Apples of gold. It's that time of year again, when we see apples of all sorts all around us— golden, red, green, crimson. They are on trees, filling the bins of the produce section in grocery stores, filling baskets in front of rustic looking places like farms or old-fashioned restaurants, or on the covers and inside pages of magazines. Nothing makes me feel quite like the fall/winter holidays as much as apples. They are a delight to the eye, this time of year or any time, for that matter. Solomon uses them to paint a mental picture of how beautiful words can be when spoken at the right time.

All of my four children sucked their thumbs as babies, but my second one seemed to love it the most. He even sucked his thumb in the womb. I saw it on an ultrasound!

Getting him to stop was a challenge. The other children seemed to simply outgrow the habit—but not this child. At nearly four, he still walked around with his thumb in his mouth non-stop. Finally, I decided I had to start discouraging the practice. I read somewhere it works well to have a child cut down on his thumb-sucking habit before stopping altogether. This can be accomplished by restricting thumb sucking during waking hours while still allowing it at bedtime or naptime.

I explained this to my son. I told him not to suck his thumb except at special times, like bedtime or naptime. After a few weeks the verbal reminders began to work and soon my child was completely free of the habit during waking hours.

One day, my friend, Laura, offered to take my children for their allergy shots along with her children who also needed them. That day as the children played in the doctor's office waiting room, this son, slid down the plastic slide a little too hard. He landed with a thump and apparently hurt himself upon impact with the floor, so he began to cry loudly.

Soon his cries turned into screams and he refused to be comforted. Laura tried everything she could think of. She tried holding him on her lap and loving him. She tried talking gently to him, but also to no avail. My son's screams grew louder, so

Laura tried a different tactic. She scolded him a little, telling him he was not hurt badly, and he needed to stop crying!

Finally, in desperation, with the entire waiting room watching to see how she would handle the situation, she told my son in no uncertain terms that continuing to cry was simply not acceptable! This didn't work either and he kept on as loudly as ever. Completely out of ideas, Laura turned to my oldest son who was about seven at the time. She asked him if he had any ideas. This son, who had been playing quietly throughout the entire episode, stood up from his chair and walked slowly toward his little brother. He put his arm around his little brother's shoulder and softly said, "You know how Mommy says you can only suck your thumb at special times? Well, this is one of those times."

With that, the younger brother stuck his much-loved thumb into his mouth and the crying stopped instantly!

I'm sure the peaceful silence after such a long episode of crying was as beautiful to the waiting room of people as apples of gold in pictures of silver!

The passage in James portrays a very different

picture of words that can come out of our mouths—
words we utter with our tongue. James tells us that
the tongue can be a fire. It can defile our entire
body. He draws a striking contrast in how easy it is
to tame wild animals compared to taming the
tongue, for with our mouths we can utter both
blessings and curses.

I have to ask myself, how am I using my
words? Is my tongue a fire? Is it defiling everything
else about me? When people think of me do they
remember mean, angry, harsh things I have said, or
do they feel encouraged by my words? What about
you? Are your words timely and wise, calming,
encouraging, and uplifting others? Are we using
our mouths to tell others about the goodness of our
God? Are others drawn to us and our God like
people would be drawn to apples of gold in pictures
of silver, or do they avoid us for fear of being
burned by our words like one would want to keep
his or her distance from a fire?

As I ponder the striking contrast in how my
tongue can be used, I am reminded of another Bible
verse. It reads like a prayer: "May these words of
my mouth and this meditation of my heart be
pleasing in your sight, LORD, my Rock and my

Redeemer" (Psalm 19:14).

May God help our words become apples of gold for His glory!

Prayer: Heavenly Father, teach us to guard our tongues so that they may be used for Your glory. Like my son's words to his brother, may our words stop the crying around us and bring comfort to others. In Jesus' name, Amen.

Thought for the Day: When you see the beautiful apples this holiday season, let them remind you to use your words wisely.

Prepare Your Heart for Thanksgiving
by Shirley
Read: Ephesians 6:10-20

Put on the whole armor of God,
that you may be able
to stand against the schemes of the devil.
Ephesians 6:11

In October of one year, while enjoying supper and fellowship with two friends, we began talking about how quickly Thanksgiving would be upon us. One of the friends relayed how much she dreaded Thanksgiving because of all the family drama. The other friend talked about how excited she was that it would not be long before she saw all her family, but she admitted it was a stressful time.

Many variations of these thoughts and emotions wash over us as we begin to think about the upcoming holidays, don't they?

What do you most look forward to about Thanksgiving? What do you most dread? What can you do to make your family's Thanksgiving better?

Many of us desire our Thanksgiving to consist of meaningful interactions with our family and friends that make sweet lasting memories. And, as Christ-followers, we want to be truly thankful for and during our Thanksgiving celebrations.

Often a person who dreads Thanksgiving thinks the solution to the problem is for someone else to change, but we know that often the change actually needs to begin with the person who is dreading the holiday.

As Christ-followers we must prepare our hearts by continually going to the Lord in prayer, reading the Bible, being sensitive to the Holy Spirit's conviction of our own sinful thoughts and attitudes, being quick to repent of sin and walk in the strength of God's forgiveness. It is easy to let our time with God slip when our schedules begin to fill, but do not forego your set-aside time with the Lord.

When we are in the throes of planning for Thanksgiving, many of us just go into automatic pilot mode and don't take time to pray for the Lord's guidance and strength.

It is helpful for me to remember some important truths about Thanksgiving. A note I wrote in the margin of my Bible beside 1 Chronicles 16:34 says, "Thanksgiving is Trinitarian." How so? Thanksgiving is when we give thanks to God, which we do through prayer.

We pray to the Father, through the Son, in the Holy Spirit. The Trinity is built into our Thanksgiving and our daily lives.

Often, the main focus of our Thanksgiving gets lost in all the trimmings and hoopla. The primary focus of our gratitude and prayers of thanksgiving is "the grace of God that was given you in Christ Jesus" (1 Corinthians 1:4). Remember, "God shows his love for us in that while we were still sinners, Christ died for us" (Romans 5:8).

Today's passage gives us great insight into preparing for Thanksgiving and everything else that lies ahead. The short answer is to pray "at all times in the Spirit" as we put on the whole armor of God: the belt of truth, the breastplate of righteousness, shoes—readiness given by the gospel of peace, the shield of faith, helmet of salvation, and the sword of the Spirit (Ephesians 6:10-20).

If you don't already keep a prayer journal, start one now. Numerous times a day record all the things for which you are thankful and remember to actually stop and thank God for each of them!

If there is any friction between family members or others who will be with you during your Thanksgiving feast, begin now to pray about each situation. Pray that the Lord would soften hardened hearts (including your own), give each person a heart of love and forgiveness, and lead each person to repent of sin where it is present. And, the Apostle Paul tells us to replace sin with thanksgiving (Ephesians 5:4).

The bottom line is that we are to give thanks—not just during the Thanksgiving holiday—but every moment of every day. We must continually prepare our hearts so that we can be thankful people at all times and in all situations.

Prayer: Thank You Heavenly Father for the amazing blessings and gifts You shower upon us. Help me to develop a thankful heart so that my thanksgiving to You flows unhindered. In Jesus' name, Amen.

Thought for the Day: Get dressed and ready for battle, I mean, Thanksgiving.

Gathered Fragments

by Harriet
Read: Isaiah 61:1-3, Psalm 147:3

*And when they had eaten their fill,
he told his disciples,
"Gather up the leftover fragments,
that nothing may be lost."
John 6:12*

I first noticed this verse in an old handwritten book my father has on his shelf. It was handed down to him by his mother who got it from her mother. It appears to be an old journal of some type. On the pages of the book are poems gathered and carefully written by its first owner. Some are famous poems while others are original work by family members. My grandmother and even my father have some original poems handwritten by them in this treasured book. The book is titled, *Gathered Fragments* and this verse is written in beautiful penmanship on the first page.

These words in Scripture were actually an instruction by Jesus to His disciples after the miraculous feeding of five thousand people. The crowd which gathered to hear Jesus was hungry. It was lunchtime, and the people were without food.

Most of them had gathered spontaneously without planning ahead even enough to have brought lunches. Rather than going home, the disciples found a little boy with a small lunch of five loaves of bread and two small fish. After blessing the food, Jesus broke it into pieces, and offered it to the hungry crowd who consumed it eagerly. Then, when the crowd had eaten all they wanted, the disciples were told to gather up the fragments, that nothing be lost.

Isn't that a beautiful instruction? I am reminded of it every fall when the squirrels scamper all around gathering up nuts to store for the winter.

How do you gather fragments? Do you keep old photos and relics polished and put in a place of honor? Perhaps you give them away as special gifts? My father has a plaque hanging in his home of an old letter he wrote to his mother from camp when he was a child. His sister found the letter and made a very special birthday gift for him one year. Maybe you have carefully held onto family heirlooms so you can pass them to the next generation. Or perhaps, you gather fragments in other ways. Maybe you freeze fruits and vegetables for winter meals, or maybe you gather and dry herbs, fruits, or vegetables.

There are so many ways to gather fragments. Through the years, I have learned another way. I have had more than one occasion to help gather the fragments of a loved one's shattered life. I find myself drawn to the gathering role. While others are shattering through accusations, anger, or gossip, my heart aches and longs to help the broken friend or family member to gather his or her life back together. I remember how God has gathered my broken life and put it back together so many times.

Our focal passages speak to this. The Psalms passage lets us know that God is a fragment gatherer, too, as He puts people's lives back together. He heals the broken hearted and binds up their wounds.

What or who needs gathering in your life? What or who is in danger of being lost? Perhaps the shattered, broken life or lives are not people you know. Maybe you learn from the news of others, even groups of people, whose lives have been shattered, and your heart longs to help in whatever way you can. Even if it's through donations, you are still helping to "gather up the leftover fragments, that nothing be lost" (John 6:12).

Even when we do simple, seemingly fun things like keeping scrapbooks, or framing old family pictures, we are keeping the heritage of those who came before from being lost—we are gathering fragments. May we be aware of the things around us that need to be gathered. May we always remember Jesus' instructions to "gather up the fragments, that nothing be lost."

When the disciples gathered the fragments in the Bible story, they gathered twelve baskets full of leftovers. Though this was a miraculous occurrence, the underlying principle is still valid. If you or I form fragment-gathering habits, we will find abundance in our lives, too. And so will others whom we bless with our fragments—carefully gathered and lovingly given.

Prayer: Loving Father, use us in the lives of broken people. Show us ways we can minister and share Your love to these shattered lives around us. And in the times when it is our lives that shatter, draw close to us, binding our wounds, and touching us with Your healing hands. In Jesus' name, Amen.

Thought for the Day: Learn to be a fragment gatherer.

Chapter 2: Honoring Veterans

Do You Still Remember the Sacrifice?

by Shirley
Read: Hebrews 9:23-28

Greater love has no one than this,
that one lay down his life for his friends.
John 15:13

Do you still remember the heroes who sacrificed their lives so that our nation would remain free? Or, do you only pull out those patriotic memories and feelings on patriotic holidays? Do you still remember the sacrifice of our courageous military men and women?

Total commitment is what President Abraham Lincoln had in mind when he spoke these words during the dedication of the Soldiers' National Cemetery at Gettysburg, Pennsylvania, November 19, 1863:

> "Four score and seven years ago our fathers brought forth on this continent, a new nation, conceived in liberty, and dedicated to the proposition that all men are created equal."

President Lincoln helped the audience be

cognizant of the heroes' sacrifice as they remembered the past, recognized the present situation, and looked to the future. They were reminded of the reasons for breaking ties with England and signing the Declaration of Independence that established the new nation, under God, upon the concept of "life, liberty and the pursuit of happiness." The President explained that the "great civil war," as he called it, was being fought to test the country's ability to endure.

Lincoln reminded them of the unfinished work of the nation and admonished the living to dedicate themselves to continue the work so that this "nation, under God" would endure and not "perish from the earth."

Are you still remembering the sacrifice of our merciful Savior? Just as President Lincoln's address prompted his audience to remember the past, recognize the present situation, and look to the future, we as Christ-followers must do the same.

Before we became Christ-followers, we were sinful people at odds with Holy God—we were spiritually dead! Through His sacrificial death on the cross, sinless Jesus Christ stepped in and did what we could not do. Now, Christ-followers are redeemed, free to live as His children, new creations being transformed by the power of the Holy Spirit as we rest in the finished work of Christ. And, we have the glorious assurance of eternal life with Christ!

What must we remember about sacrifice? The unfinished work of our nation will not be completed by America's military. President Ronald Reagan said, "… We are resolved to stand firm against those who would destroy the freedoms we cherish …."

Each one of us must also sacrifice as we fight the subtle war that threatens our nation, the spiritual, economic, and political battles we face daily to maintain the often taken for granted freedoms we now enjoy.

Thankfully, the work of our redemption in Christ Jesus is finished! However, we must remain cognizant of the ultimate sacrifice—Jesus Christ—who gave His life so that in Him we would have freedom that brings eternal life as well as freedom to walk in the newness of life through the power of the Holy Spirit. 1 Corinthians 16:13 tells us to, "Be on the alert, stand firm in the faith, act like men, be strong" (NKJV).

Prayer: Heavenly Father, thank You for the sacrifice of Jesus on the cross that purchased my pardon from sin and ensures my eternal life. I pray that I would be mindful of the sacrifice of men and women throughout history who have fought to allow our nation to worship You freely. I pray that You would ignite a revival in my heart that would spread throughout my family, city, state, nation, and the world. In Jesus' name, Amen.

Thought for the Day: As our grateful response for the sacrifice of Christ, we present ourselves as living sacrifices to God (Romans 12:1), giving Him 100% of ourselves as we serve Him.

Send me, Lord

by Harriet
Read: Romans 10:14-15, Isaiah 6:8

Jonathan said to his young armor-bearer,
"Come, let's go ...
Nothing can hinder the LORD from saving,
whether by many or by few. "
1 Samuel 14:6 (NKJV)

Molly Pitcher was only twenty-four years old when she became a Revolutionary War heroine in the Battle of Monmouth. She was at the scene of the battle because she, along with other soldiers' wives, did the work of carrying water to their husbands on the battle field. This was not because the soldiers were unusually thirsty. No, this water was important for more than just keeping the soldiers hydrated. In those days, water was used to cool down the cannons after each shot. Molly, whose real name was Mary Ludwig Hays, became one of the "water girls" in the Battle of Monmouth. That's how she got her nickname. Molly was a common nickname for a woman named Mary back in those days, and when the men needed someone to bring them a pitcher of water for their cannons, they would yell, "Molly! Pitcher!"

In June 1778, at the Battle of Monmouth, Molly attended the soldiers in her role of water carrier. It was quite hot that day, with temperatures reaching above 100 degrees Fahrenheit. The Continental Army fought in this intense heat and suffered great losses. At one-point Molly's husband collapsed at his cannon and had to be carried off the battle field. When this happened, Molly stepped up and began firing his cannon for him. She continued to man this cannon and to bravely fight alongside the men until the British were pushed back.

In her later years, after her husband had passed away and she had remarried, Mary Ludwig Hays McCauley, a.k.a. Molly Pitcher, was recognized by the Commonwealth of Pennsylvania for her heroism in battle and given a pension for her services in the Continental army.

When the need arose, and the cry rang out, "Who can man the cannon?" Molly Pitcher responded with, "Here am I. I'll help."

In today's key verse, the prophet Isaiah hears a similar question. His is not a call to battle, but rather a call to evangelize. He hears God's voice asking who will do His will? In the case of Isaiah that will was to evangelize, but sometimes God may be asking something else of us—who will minister, who will teach, or who will worship?

I have to ask myself, how do I respond when I perceive a need? What about you? How do you and I react when we feel God nudging at our hearts, when we feel Him asking, "Who will do this or that for Me?" Do we remain silent assuming someone else will answer God's call? Maybe we even run and hide in the hopes that He won't notice us? Or do we step up to the plate like Molly Pitcher did when she was needed on the battlefield? She had so many things that could have kept her from doing what she did, like intense heat, concern for her husband, and even just being a woman at that time in history. Can you imagine trying to man a cannon under those circumstances? Just having to do that wearing a long dress might have been enough to discourage me. Or do we respond with a willing heart? Do we answer like Molly and the prophet Isaiah saying, "Here am I. I'll help; send me."

Prayer: Lord, open our eyes to see the needs around us and give us hearts willing to help. Show us Your will and help us to say, "Here am I Lord. Use me." In your Son's name, Amen.

Thought for the Day: Opportunities happen every day!

At the Gates

by Harriet
Read: Matthew 16:13-18

... on this rock I will build my church,
and the gates of Hades will not overcome it.
Matthew 16:18 (NIV)

"The enemy is at the gates!"

If you were a soldier taking refuge in a fortified camp, what would you think if you heard these words? Would they strike fear in your heart?

The phrase implies that an invading army has the upper hand in the battle. We know this because they are storming the gates of the defending army. The invading army is on the attack putting the other army on defense.

On June 6, 1944, a historic day also known as D-Day during World War II, the Allied forces held an offense such as described above when they stormed the shores of Normandy, France, in what became known as the Battle of Normandy. This difficult and bloody battle, that lasted nearly a month, was the start of the Allied invasion of northwest Europe. The storming of the shores of Normandy in this battle became the single largest amphibious operation in history. Despite large casualties, the invasion was successful, and the Allied armies were able to commence the Western European campaign and start the march to Germany to take down the Nazi regime.

In this strategic battle, the Allied armies mounted a strong offensive attack.

That is the picture we see in today's Scripture—one of a winning army storming the gates of a defensive, losing army. But look closely at the words in Matthew 16:18. Who is on the offense and who is on the defense in this verse?

Jesus said these words just after Simon Peter had made a profound statement of faith. Jesus had just asked the disciples who people said He was and followed the question with another question—who did the disciples say He was? Peter answered this second question with a bold proclamation that Jesus was "the Christ, the Son of the living God" (Matthew 16:16).

Jesus responded telling Peter, "… this was not revealed to you by flesh and blood, but by my Father in heaven. And I tell you that you are Peter, and on this rock I will build my church, and the gates of Hades will not overcome it" (Matthew 16:17-18). The name Peter meant "rock." His name before this had been Simon but Jesus renamed him to Peter—the rock.

What was the rock on which Christ was going to build His kingdom? The rock was faith in Him as the Christ, the Son of the Living God, the very kind of faith that Peter had just demonstrated. On that type of faith Jesus would build His church—an offensive invading army that would knock down the very gates of Hades, or hell, overcoming it by His blood. Revelation 12:11 tells us the weapons used by this army, by which they overcome hell itself. It says they overcame "by the blood of the Lamb and by the word of their testimony; they did not love their lives so much as to shrink from death."

We need not be frightened when we feel like we are losing in a spiritual battle of some sort. The truth is, we are on the winning side. We are the offensive force. Like the Allied forces when they stormed the shores of Normandy, we are storming hell's gates and because of the blood of the Lamb, the word of our testimonies, and our commitment to the cause of Christ, even if it costs our lives, we will prevail!

Prayer: Father, You are a stronghold and are mighty in battle. Encourage us with Your word and Your Spirit that we may continue engaging in battle knowing that our victory is assured. In Your Son's name, Amen.

Thought for the Day: We are on the march and the gates of hell will not stand against us.

A Marine Explains Sacrifice

by Shirley
Read: Hebrews 9:24-28

*But as it is, he appeared once for all
at the end of the ages
to put away sin by the sacrifice of himself.*
Hebrews 9:26

One cold November morning, I stopped at a fast-food restaurant for breakfast and to prepare for a Bible study I would be teaching that evening. Two men sat at a table across from me, one probably in his early 90s and the other in his 30s. The elderly gentleman was in a wheelchair, his voice raspy, his gray hair yellowed, his skin weathered and wrinkled. They were talking about the Veteran's Day parade they hoped to be able to enjoy later that day. (Birmingham, Alabama has the oldest and largest in the country).

I was typing notes on my laptop until I overheard the following exchange. I began typing furiously so I could remember what I heard. Their slow southern drawls helped me get it all down.

"I wish I could march, or even shuffle, in the parade. Guess those days are long gone," the elderly man said wistfully.

"You couldn't pay me enough to walk all that way," proclaimed the younger man.

"I would give almost everything but my soul to march alongside my fellow veterans," replied the elderly man.

The young man said, "Your soul? What do mean?"

The elderly man perked up a bit, "Your soul is the sum of your heart and mind. It is that part that Jesus Christ died on the cross and was resurrected to save from eternal death."

"Pops you are a strange old man, but I love you," the young man retorted.

Tears began streaming down Pops' cheeks, which seemed to make the younger man extremely uncomfortable, "Come on Pops, quit crying. Let's enjoy our breakfast and not have another one of our discussions."

"Mike (not his real name), I don't want a discussion, I want you to listen carefully to your great-granddaddy. It is so sad that you do not understand what sacrifice is."

"Yes, I do!" protested Mike.

"Please listen. You see, if you understood real sacrifice, you would want the privilege of marching alongside those who had sacrificed and put their lives on hold to serve in the military; to march with those who were not killed during a war. Their sacrifice is worthy of our gratitude and respect.

"If you understood the battles that were fought, you would understand sacrifice. Military men and women fought to give you and your children the freedoms we enjoy in America. The most important of these freedoms, not that we will have it for long though, is the freedom to sit here in the open and talk with you about my Lord and Savior Jesus Christ, to freely worship Him."

Mike shot one of those dismissive "here he goes again" looks.

Pops lovingly admonished, "Mike, I know you don't want to believe there is a God who is over all things and sent His only Son to die on the cross, but He did! Because of His death and resurrection all those who believe on Him as Savior and Lord will be free from the hold of Satan, the bondage of sin, and eternal punishment in hell."

"Pops, I thought we were talking about Veteran's Day, not God!"

"Can't talk about Veteran's Day without talking about sacrifice. Can't talk about sacrifice without talking about the greatest sacrifice, Jesus. The sacrifice of veterans is a picture, flawed and incomplete as it is, of Christ's sacrifice on the cross. Christ died to take our sin and punishment, so we can walk in the freedom of God's grace. Veterans served, and many gave their lives so that Americans can walk in the freedom we have in America. Until we, the American people, come to understand that God is in control and that He is to be worshiped, praised, and served, our freedom will be incomplete!"

As I left for work, I stooped down so I was eyeball-to-eyeball with Pops and asked, "In what branch did you serve?"

"I'm a Marine!" he proudly replied.

I told him my dad was a Navy corpsman attached to the 3rd Marine Division on Iwo Jima and Guam and said, "Thank you for your service to our country, and more importantly, our God!"

"Semper Fi!" Pops said in a raspy, broken voice.

Several people around us began standing and applauding. I turned his wheelchair so he could see what was happening. As he looked around, different ones nodded and said, "Thank you."

Prayer: Gracious Heavenly Father, thank You for the sacrifice You gave of Jesus Your Son to take my sin upon Himself and the punishment I deserve so that I may live in the freedom of Your forgiveness. Thank You that through the sacrifice of many women and men we live in a nation where we can worship You freely. In Jesus' name, Amen.

Thought for the Day: Remember that great sacrifice is required for you to live in freedom—in Christ and in America.

Change and Uncertainty

by Harriet
Read: Psalm 37:23-26

*The LORD makes firm the steps of one
who delights in Him.
Psalm 37:23 (NIV)*

I have experienced war. No, I am not a veteran, but nonetheless, I have lived through a war, for at least a couple of years of my life. I experienced it as a child in Nigeria. I never actually fought in battle, but the ravages of war have touched me. I have seen people I love in danger for their lives and learned what it is to be afraid. I have seen armed soldiers on the streets, been stopped at roadblocks, and known the fear of my father being sent to a dangerous area. He was not sent to that area to fight, but rather to help the hospital stay open. When our mission board evacuated the permanent personnel at this station in the dark of night under gunfire, they asked the other doctors, like my dad, to take turns serving for short periods at that hospital, which was quite close to the battle lines. I know how war can impact a person, forever.

In November 2011, a man by the name of Chukwuemeka Odumegwu Ojukwu passed away in a London hospital at the age of 78. That name may mean nothing to many people, but the man changed my world. To me, he was General Ojukwu, a household name in my childhood home in Nigeria, in the mid-late 1960s.

In 1966, I was a little girl playing happily in the Nigerian town of Ogbomoso. I had trees to climb in, sprawling green grass to run on, pet monkeys and parrots to play with, yummy oranges and guavas I could pick right off the trees in my backyard, and friends I loved. Except for having to look out for critters, some possibly dangerous, my world was safe. But also in 1966, unbeknownst to me, this man, General Ojukwu, declared a part of Nigeria to be the sovereign nation of Biafra, causing a civil war.

I learned new words—like hate, war, fear, danger. I saw Awudi, my beloved nanny, sent away because she was of the Igbo tribe and from the eastern part of the nation—the part that was trying to become Biafra. My parents told me people might want to harm her just because she belonged to that particular tribe. I could not understand why anyone would want to harm another person because of something they could not control, like the color of their skin or the tribe to which they belonged. To me, Awudi was the embodiment of love. I couldn't imagine anyone wanting to harm her for any reason, especially people who did not even know her. Finally, in 1968 my parents left Nigeria forever and I learned other terms—separation, loss, and sadness.

It's funny how one person's life impacts another. I never knew General Ojukwu personally. Some thought he was a hero, others thought he was a villain. All I know is that the man changed the trajectory of my life forever. However, when I think back on things, I am not sad because my Lord was directing my steps all along, even using sad experiences like war, loss, and separation.

I am reminded of some words from the prophet Isaiah. In Isaiah 6:1 he writes, "In the year that King Uzziah died, I saw the Lord high and exalted, seated on a throne; and the train of his robe filled the temple."

A time of a king's death would naturally have been a time of change and uncertainty for the people whom he had ruled. Yet, what was Isaiah's reaction to the uncertainty of what must have been political change all around him? He saw the Lord, high and lifted up! He saw an eternal truth—that no matter the circumstances we face here on earth, God is still on His throne in perfect control of things. May we learn to keep our eyes on Him no matter what changes are occurring in our lives today!

Prayer: Heavenly Father, You are above all things and in control of all things. Thank You for making firm the steps of Your people through all the circumstances of life! In Your Son's name, Amen.

Thought for the Day: Even in times of change and uncertainty, God makes your steps firm if you delight in Him!

Chapter 3: Here Come the Holidays

The Apple of His Eye

by Harriet
Read: Psalm 17:6-8

Keep me as the apple of your eye;
hide me in the shadow of your wings.
Psalm 17:8 (NIV)

Shirley's mother was my Aunt Jeannie. She
was not my real aunt; she was my missionary aunt.
Growing up on the mission field, we missionary
kids (or MKs as we were called) all referred to each
other's parents as aunt or uncle. And we all felt like
we were some kind of a mix between best friends,
siblings, and cousins. After all, our biological
aunts, uncles, and cousins were half a world away
across a vast ocean. But we never felt like we
missed out on anything. We loved our adopted
family and our adopted homeland. We spent our
days playing under palm trees beneath the tropical
sun, and we had more aunts, uncles, and cousins
than we could count.

So, this precious woman was my "Aunt
Jeannie" for as far back as I can remember.
Shirley's family lived directly across the dirt road
from me in our little town of Ogbomoso, Nigeria.
Being so close in proximity, I was also emotionally

close to Aunt Jeannie.

She radiated God's love! Though she faced dark and difficult circumstances many times in her life, Aunt Jeannie always held fast to her faith. In her old age, for many years until God took her home, I was blessed to see her at least once a year at our annual missionary reunions. She always greeted me with a huge smile, her arms wide open, and praises to God on her lips.

A few years before God called her home, Aunt Jeannie and Shirley came to my home for Thanksgiving. There was another missionary aunt and uncle whom Shirley and I have known our whole lives living in the same city as I do. This precious couple, their daughter, my parents, husband and children, Shirley, and Aunt Jeannie all shared the Thanksgiving meal for several years in a row. What great memories! We told old stories, reminisced of our lives on the mission field and laughed until we cried. Aunt Jeannie could tell hilarious stories, and one year she even danced a little jig for us in spite of her failing health. She was a truly special woman, and I was so blessed to have called her my aunt all those years.

When I think of Aunt Jeannie, I think of a

certain expression I heard her say many, many times. She would talk about the goodness of her Savior and then she would say, "God loves all of His children you know … but I'm His favorite."

Sitting next to the festive Thanksgiving table, Aunt Jeannie would get that twinkle in her eyes as she paused just long enough for what she said to sink in. Then, pointing to me as she spoke, she would add softly, "… And so are you."

The first time I heard her say this, it delighted me. Aunt Jeannie was right, you know. She was her Father's favorite, and so am I … and so are you. God would have sent Jesus if it had only been for me, or for you. There are so many passages in the Bible which tell of God's great love for us. Today's verse says we are the apple of His eye.

Prayer: Father, thank You for keeping us as the apple of Your eye. Thank You for lavishing Your love upon us! In Jesus' name, Amen.

Thought for the Day: As the old hymn goes, "Jesus loves me, this I know. For the Bible tells me so."

Beauty is in the Eye of the Beholder

by Shirley
Read: 1 John 3:1-3

One thing I ask from the Lord, this only do I seek:
that I may dwell in the house of the Lord
all the days of my life, to gaze on the beauty
of the Lord and to seek him in his temple.
Psalm 27:4 (NIV)

It was my privilege to live with my mom during the final years of her life. When I came home late at night, she would be in bed dozing until she knew I had arrived safely at home. My routine was to go into her room, give her a kiss on her forehead and say, "Goodnight Mom, I love you." She would reach out to give me a big hug, then a kiss on my cheek, and without fail, she would say, "I love you! How do you manage to look so beautiful after such a long day?" This always tickled me so much because the lights were off, and the room would be pitch black!

Sometimes when we were telling stories and laughing with friends, I would poke fun at her for telling me how beautiful I looked when it was so dark in the room that she could not even see me. Whenever I did, she would get that let-me-set-you-straight look on her face, point to her eyes, and explain, "I don't have to see you with these eyes to know you are beautiful." She would then begin patting over her heart. "I see you through these eyes, and you are beautiful!" My mom, the beholder, was viewing me through the eyes of her heart with which she dearly loved me; therefore, she saw beauty.

When we look at the beautiful Thanksgiving, Christmas, and New Year decorations with only our physical eyes, we miss seeing the spectacularly exquisite beauty that flows from the foundation and backdrop of our celebration and makes each decoration meaningful.

What is this spectacularly exquisite beauty?

It is the gospel, the good news. It is the beauty Christ-followers behold with the eyes of redeemed hearts—God's grace, mercy, love, and justice. The eyes of redeemed hearts behold the birth of a baby born in a very simple stable and placed in a manger as the continuing story of God redeeming and restoring His people. They behold the continuing story when, on the cross, that grown baby takes their sin upon Himself, receives the punishment they deserve and dies on that cross. They behold

His burial, resurrection, and then His ascension to heaven where He now sits at the right hand of the throne of God Almighty. Through faith these eyes behold their eternal life, glorifying Him forever!

As we behold every Thanksgiving, Christmas, and New Year decoration through the eyes of our redeemed hearts, we see in each and every one the spectacularly exquisite beauty of God's love for His children. These decorations remind us of God's gift of salvation that brings us into a relationship through which we are formed into His image in preparation for spending eternity with Him in heaven. These decorations merely foreshadow the spectacularly exquisite beauty we shall behold when we see our Lord and Savior Jesus Christ face-to-face!

Prayer: Our Gracious Heavenly Father, You are the creator of beauty. You placed it in Your world and deep in our souls. Thank You for the eternal beauty that is ours in Christ Jesus. In His name, Amen.

Thought for the Day: There is no beauty like God's spectacularly exquisite beauty!

Blessed Indeed!

by Harriet
Read: Luke 1:41-45

*And blessed is she who believed that there
would be a fulfillment of what had been
spoken to her by the Lord.
Luke 1:45 (NASB)*

"It's Christmas time!"

Hearing that exclamation conjures up a myriad of thoughts ... family, gifts, snow, savory smells from the kitchen, fires burning in the fireplace, frost on the window, and tinsel glistening from a decorated tree. For Christians it also reminds us of something else—the gift God gave us when He sent His Son, born into this world as a tiny baby. When we think of the Christmas narrative, the usual people come to mind, Mary, Joseph, the shepherds, angels, wise men, and of course, the baby Jesus.

Sometimes, after we have thought of all of these, we remember Mary's cousin Elizabeth and how her baby leapt inside of her at the presence of Jesus. But as for me, it now reminds me of Elizabeth every time I hear it—ever since that fall.

It was late fall, the end of October to be exact, many years ago now. I was consumed with concern for a family member who was going through the greatest emotional struggle of her life. She had suffered a trauma that left her reeling and struggling to survive in its aftermath. I had spent so many days, weeks, and even months praying fervently for her; I had agonized in prayer for her. And thankfully, through seeking God and reading His word, I had found hope.

That October, I was attending the annual reunion of my mission family. Every fall the missionaries who served with my parents and Shirley's parents in Nigeria, gather for a reunion. We meet at a conference center in the beautiful Alabama mountains for a time of refreshing and sweet fellowship. We attend services, fellowship around the tables at the meals, and enjoy activities with each other. It is always one of the highlights of my year!

But that year, my hurting family member was heavy on my mind. I shared her story with one of my childhood friends telling her about the situation as well as the hope God had given to me in spite of the circumstances.

"Blessed is she who believes there would be a fulfillment of what had been spoken to her by the

Lord," my friend said immediately. She explained further, "It's a Bible verse. It comes from Luke 1:45 and is part of Elizabeth's song of praise to the Lord." My friend smiled as she spoke.

She went on to tell me that this was a favorite verse of hers because it uses the pronoun she. So many verses use he, but this one says, "Blessed is she who believes there would be a fulfillment of what had been spoken to her by the Lord," my friend pointed out. Then she encouraged me to hang on to the assurance and hope I had found.

That was many years ago. My family member pulled through and is now well. Being a woman, I treasure this verse, too. It has become a favorite verse of mine, too. Ever since that fall, I cannot think of Christmas without remembering Elizabeth and this verse.

Prayer: Thank You, Lord, for the promises in Your word. Thank You that You will fulfill them in Your timing. Give us the faith to believe You. In Your Son's name, Amen.

Thought for the Day: God lavishes His blessings on women and men who believe His word.

The Light of the World

by Shirley
Read: John 1:9-13

Again Jesus spoke to them, saying
"I am the light of the world.
Whoever follows me will not walk in darkness,
but will have the light of life."
John 8:12

Today's passage points us to the Light of the World—Jesus—who brings hope for people who are dead in their trespasses and sin, and struggling in the darkness of disappointment, failure, illness, and difficult situations.

A social media post prompted a long conversation with a friend about God and my mom. In the post, I wrote: "She was just an 'ordinary' woman in so many ways, yet, extraordinary in so many other ways."

For those who knew my mom, ordinary is not a word that usually comes to mind when they think of her. Yet, she was ordinary in so many ways. My mom was the eighth child of nine children born to my grandparents. She always described herself as an ordinary, awkward, bucktoothed girl who was always the clown!

In her childhood and teens, she struggled to fit in at school and had grandiose dreams of what she wanted to do in her life and the places she wanted to go. She did laundry, cooked meals, ironed and mended clothes, did the grocery shopping, doctored a gazillion boo-boos, and kissed away her children's fears and hurts. She got angry at and hurt by people and circumstances, dealt with the effects of aging on her body and health, and experienced a myriad of disappointments. Like some of our lives, Mom's life wasn't easy in many ways.

So why is it that such an ordinary woman is remembered by so many people across the world as extraordinary?

In the midst of hardships, disappointments, fear, and great loss, Mom would pray, "Lord God, strengthen me so that all those watching will know that You alone are my strength and hope." That prayer was often followed by her singing, "The Light of the World is Jesus" (Philip P. Bliss):

"No darkness have we who in Jesus abide;
The Light of the world is Jesus!
We walk in the light when we follow our Guide!
The Light of the world is Jesus!

Come to the Light, 'tis shining for thee;
Sweetly the Light has dawned upon me.
Once I was blind, but now I can see:
The Light of the world is Jesus!"

Although her singing voice in her latter years was raspy and a bit off-tune, in those moments as she prayed and sang, there would not be a movement or a sound from anyone within earshot or eyesight, as this ordinary woman led everyone to look to Jesus (Hebrews 12:1-2) the Light of the World.

How was it possible for Mom to lead people to have such strong faith and to exhibit the joy of the Lord in and through every circumstance?

My friend Chuck Wall, in teaching about reflecting Jesus, used a mirror as his illustration. He held up a mirror and asked the young people to tell him what they say saw. They kept naming all things they saw reflected in the mirror, but not one specific thing. He kept asking, "What else?" Finally, he told them they had not said they saw the mirror itself. The point of this illustration was to reiterate that as Christ-followers, we are not to draw attention to ourselves, but we are to reflect our Savior so fully that people see Jesus, and not us. That is precisely why, when people looked at this "ordinary" woman, my mom, they saw the work of an extraordinary God shine in and through her because she knew, loved, and obediently served Him!

Prayer: Father, we thank You for sending the Light of the World, Jesus, to this dark and sin-filled world, to bring the light of the gospel to us! Give us a passion to know You better so that in the midst of our lives we can be a shining light showing the world who You are. In Jesus' name we pray, Amen.

Thought for the Day: Knowing Jesus, the Light of the World, gives us hope for living day to day.

Life's Ripples

by Harriet
Read: Psalm 74:13-17

The day is yours, and yours also the night;
you established the sun and moon.
It was you who set all the boundaries of the earth;
you made both summer and winter.
Psalm 74:16-17 (NIV)

Autumn was once an enigma to me. As a little girl growing up beneath the hot tropical sun, I had no memory of autumn. Oh, I had experienced it when my parents were in America on furlough, but I was too young to really remember what it was like. And furlough when you are only five years old is a year of so many new things, that it is hard to process and remember.

But nonetheless, even in tropical Nigeria, I learned to love the autumn season. Why did I love it as a child when I had not experienced it? Where did I get my love for this season of cooler weather, colorful scenery, scurrying squirrels, crunchy leaves, and frosty mornings? I think the credit goes to a missionary aunt who taught both Shirley and me in school—our Aunt Lil Wasson.

Because she had a teaching degree and several

children of her own in need of an education, Aunt Lil bravely took on the job of elementary school teacher to all the missionary kids on the Ogbomoso compound. Ogbomoso, the Nigerian town where we lived, had both a hospital and seminary with about a half-dozen missionary families working in each. All together these missionaries had at least a dozen or more elementary age children, depending on who was on furlough in any given year. Aunt Lil taught all of us in her garage which had been made into a one-room school house. She taught every child in grades kindergarten through the fourth grade in one room. She was a brave woman, indeed.

Aunt Lil loved autumn. She grew up in Arkansas where trees are abundant and autumns are glorious. Of course, Nigeria had only two seasons—rainy and dry. Half the year it rained some every day and the other half it did not rain at all. America's autumn months fall right at the end of rainy season in Nigeria.

Yet, Aunt Lil always decorated her schoolroom with pictures representative of autumn in America and had her American citizen students learn about their homeland. I can still remember sitting in her garage classroom looking at the decorations all around me—bright orange pumpkins, brown squirrels with nuts in their mouths, and trees with red, orange, and yellow leaves.

She had one large poster-size picture of Jack Frost painting a leaf with an artist palette of fall colors which always intrigued me. He perched on a tree branch; with one hand he held the palette and with the other he painted the leaf. Of course, we all knew Jack Frost was not real, but my imagination went wild, just the same, with thoughts of a magical place where the world turned bright with colors, where shiny, frosty crystals formed on the ground, and a little elf painted the leaves when children were not looking.

I think of Aunt Lil every fall. I thank God for her enthusiasm over the world He made, both tropical and temperate. And I realize how everything people do can have a lasting ripple effect on those around them.

Prayer: Gracious Heavenly Father, creator of this vast and beautiful world, thank You for the exquisite beauty that surrounds us whether we experience colorful autumn foliage or lovely tropical blooms. Make us mindful that our lives affect others in so many ways. May we impact them for You. In Jesus' name, Amen.

Thought for the Day: Others are watching you!

Chapter 4: Thanksgiving Day is Here!

Give Thanks!

by Harriet
Read: Psalm 100

*Enter his gates with thanksgiving and his
courts with praise; give thanks to him
and praise his name.
Psalm 100:4 (NIV)*

Thanksgiving. What thoughts does that word bring to your mind? Do you picture the act of giving thanks to God for all of the blessings He has given you, or do you envision holiday celebrations? Perhaps you picture families sitting around a table full of food. A savory baked turkey sits on a large platter in the center of the table surrounded by dishes and dishes of yummy food. Or, maybe when you hear the word you see images in your mind of the first Thanksgiving with Pilgrims and Indians enjoying an outdoor meal together.

So many different Thanksgivings through the years come to my mind. When I was a child in Nigeria, we celebrated Thanksgiving with our entire mission family. What fun it was back then! The meal was held outside on a large lush lawn of one of the mission houses. The children usually had small skits to perform, songs to present, or poems to recite. I remember a year when Shirley and I and our other classmates dressed up as Pilgrims and recited "The Pilgrims Came," a poem by Annette Wynne. It was such fun to wear that long gray skirt, white scarf-type head covering and white squared cloth collar around my neck. Then, standing next to my classmates, we recited in unison,

> "The Pilgrims came across the sea,
> And never thought of you and me:
> And yet it's very strange the way
> We think of them
> Thanksgiving Day."

We went on for two more stanzas. Even more fun than pretending to be a Pilgrim was all the yummy food that my missionary aunts and uncles brought to share around those large tables set out beneath the tropical sky. That was the year I discovered olives and deviled eggs!

Then too, other memories flood my mind of Thanksgivings in America where the leaves are brightly colored and a fire roars in the fireplace.

Thanksgiving can be such a wonderful time, but sometimes it's not so wonderful. Sometimes we find ourselves alone on this day. And, sometimes we get so busy with preparations that we forget that the real reason for the holiday is to give thanks! Some years, the turkey is undercooked or the bread burns. Some years, we are emotionally raw from a recent pain in our lives.

Whatever this Thanksgiving season might bring your way, don't lose focus of the reason for the season. No matter our circumstance, we always have something for which we can be thankful.

"Pollyanna" was a bestselling children's book written in 1913 by Eleanor Porter. Disney later turned it into a film starring Haley Mills. In the story, Pollyanna, an orphan who lived with a less-than-loving aunt, always managed to find something about which to be glad. She called it "the glad game," a challenge to try finding something to be glad about no matter the circumstances.

This year at Thanksgiving, no matter our situation, let's play the "thankful game" and find things for which we are thankful. And, let's also remember to tell our friends and loved ones how thankful we are that God placed them in our lives.

Prayer: Heavenly Father, You love us so much. You gave us life and poured out blessings upon us.

Fill our hearts with thanksgiving this week and always. In Jesus' name, Amen.

Thought for the Day: For what are you thankful?

Come Before Winter

by Harriet
Read: Matthew 25:34-36, James 1:27

Make every effort to come to me soon ...
only Luke is with me ... come before winter ...
2 Timothy 4:9-13, 21a (NASB)

Sunday was visitation day at the mission
boarding school that my older brother and sister
attended. The boarding school was in the town of
Osogbo, about an hour's drive from Ogbomoso. It
was not as many miles away as one might think, but
the narrow, pot-hole-filled dirt roads made it take
longer than perhaps it should have.

Every Sunday afternoon, my younger sister
and I piled into the family car, along with our
parents, to make the hour-long trip to see our
siblings. In spite of working full-time as a nurse at
the mission hospital by my physician father's side,
my mother always worked hard to make the weekly
visits special for her two oldest children. She
brought little gift boxes of cookies and other
goodies to them each week. I can still remember
laying my head against the car's back passenger
window while I felt the car beneath me rumbling
and bumping along African dirt roads; and how

happy my older siblings were to see their family, too!

Some of the other families lived much farther away and were not able to visit their children weekly. I always felt sorry for the missionary children whose families were too far away to make the trip as often as we did.

Have you ever been alone or separated from someone you love? I have been separated from my children when they were in college, and like my mother, I often sent them gifts or goodie boxes. Separation is not as difficult today with all the means of communication that we now have available to us.

The apostle Paul found himself alone and in prison. As he wrote the second letter to Timothy, he made several pleas for others to come visit him. Today's passage is poignant to me. Paul says only Luke is with him and then he asks for some things, if Timothy is able to visit. He asks for his cloak and his books—the cloak presumably because the weather was turning cold and the books because Paul was a learned man who loved books.

James 1:27 says that pure and undefiled religion in the sight of God is to visit orphans and widows in their distress. Notice it does not say that pure religion is to give them money. No, it says to visit them. Giving monetary gifts is helpful, too, but not at the expense of a personal visit—one where you laugh with someone or perhaps even cry with him or her—a real visit where you make a connection to another person's world.

As winter approaches, I think of Paul's cry to "come before winter." It serves as a reminder in this otherwise festive season that there are those who are suffering to whom you and I can minister.

Prayer: Heavenly Father, open our eyes to the needs of those around us. Help us to make time in our busy lives to reach out to and visit with others. Bring to our remembrance that there are people who, like Paul, may desperately need to have someone in their lives who really cares. In Your Son's name, Amen.

Thought for the Day: Let us make every effort to visit the lonely and hurting people in our midst.

Taste and See

by Harriet
Read: Psalm 34:7-9

Taste and see that the Lord is good.
Psalm 34:8a (NIV)

You walk into a kitchen where Thanksgiving dinner is being prepared. Or perhaps you are the one preparing the meal, and you walk back in after having stepped out for a minute. You are suddenly engulfed by the delicious aroma that fills the room. A turkey seasoned with sage and rosemary is baking in the oven. Bread bakes on the shelf of another part of the oven, along with broccoli casserole with cheese melting in it, and hot pecan pie. Potatoes ready to mash and simmering gravy rest on top of the stove. On the countertop are a cranberry salad and a cold pumpkin pie with whipped cream next to it, waiting to be smoothed on top. You peer at the food through the oven window; the turkey is sizzling, the broccoli casserole is bubbling, and the bread and pecan pie are browned to perfection.

Your mouth waters at the delightful smells, but still you are left only imagining how delicious these foods really are. As wonderful as these foods look, and as enticing as these smells are, you need to taste the food to truly appreciate it. These other sensations pale in comparison to what you experience when you sit down at the table for dinner and actually taste the food. Only then, when you put a piece of warm bread or a fork full of cheesy broccoli in your mouth, do you really know how good it is.

King David knew this. Well, he may not have known about our American Thanksgiving turkey dinners, and the foods that made his mouth water may have been things we have never eaten, but he knew that tasting was the best way to see how good something really was. So he tells us to "taste and see that the Lord is good." We are not just to read of God's goodness in a book or hear about it from a friend or from our pastor in a sermon on a Sunday morning. No, David tells us to taste it, to experience it!

But it begs the question; how do we experience God and taste His goodness? A closer look at the rest of Psalm 34 is helpful in explaining how we do this. The passage tells us to take refuge in the Lord (vs. 8), to fear the Lord (vs. 9), and to seek Him (vs. 10). It instructs us to listen and carefully note what the Psalmist and other writers of God's word have to say (vs. 11). The passage also tells us to keep from speaking things that are evil or deceitful (vs. 13), to turn from evil, do good, and pursue peace (vs. 14).

Look at the verbs the Psalmist uses in these verses. He says to take refuge, seek, listen, turn away from, pursue. Do you notice anything special about these verbs? They are action verbs. This then is how we *taste* God's goodness. It is a call to action, not a passive observation. We are to actively engage in a walk with our Lord.

Prayer: Father, You are good. Teach me to actively pursue You. Help me to learn how to taste Your goodness. In Jesus' name, Amen.

Thought for the Day: Tasting that the Lord is good does not happen through passive observation; it requires action.

Remember God's Blessings

by Shirley
Read: 1 Corinthians 1:4-9

*I give thanks to my God always for you because
of the grace of God that was given you
in Christ Jesus.
1 Corinthians 1:4*

Holidays are often emotionally difficult for us. The Bible tells us, and I have discovered, that giving thanks to God for His blessings during difficult times helps lessen the pain we are experiencing.

This time of year always makes me miss my parents and all of the fun holiday preparations we would enjoy. The first autumn after my dad, Ray Crowder, died, my mind was flooded with memories. Those memories were overwhelming, and I was emotionally distraught.

I was talking to a friend about my feelings and after a little while he asked me, "What two things did your dad teach you?" What? I was pouring out my heart telling him how horrible I feel, and he asks me that?

Then I thought, "Only two things?" and I quickly tried to "categorize" all the things that came to my mind.

The first, and most important thing Dad taught me was to "love the Lord [my] God with all [my] heart and with all [my] soul and with all [my] might" and, to love [my] neighbor (Deuteronomy 6:5; Matthew 22:37, 39).

Dad taught me that we all have an urgent need for the gospel to bring us to salvation and for our ongoing walk with Christ, by preaching and teaching the Bible with a passion and sense of urgency for the gospel to be heard, understood, and obeyed (Acts 3:19; 1 Corinthians 9:16).

Dad taught me to use music as an expression of worship as he taught me that music is much more than correctly played notes. He taught me that when I sit at the piano, the notes I play are my expressions of awe, love and gratitude to the Sovereign God of the Universe. He taught me to pour out my heart, in prayer and praise to the Lord, through my music (Psalm 33:3; John 4:24).

Dad demonstrated how to minister to those who were hurting spiritually, emotionally, mentally, and physically. I had countless opportunities to watch him with those whose loved one had died, or a child who had overdosed on a drug, or a person suffering from some illness, or who had lost a job. Dad was always bringing them the comfort of the Comforter (2 Corinthians 1:3-5; Ephesians 4:32).

Dad taught me that if I pointed out a problem to someone, I must be willing to hang around and help them work toward a biblical solution to the situation. He taught me that the Bible has the answers for all the issues of life (2 Timothy 3:16-17; 2 Peter 1:3).

Dad taught me to be generous with my time, talents, possessions, and monetary resources. Numerous times a week, someone would show up at the doorstep of our home, saying, "A guy told me if I need help that Ray will help me." (See Matthew 25:35-40; 1 Peter 4:10.)

Dad taught me to laugh, and maybe more importantly, to laugh at myself! Ask me about the "flowers" we planted, nurtured, and fertilized for weeks … turns out we had the healthiest weeds in the world!! And his telling of *Old Mother Hubbard* was hilarious.

Dad taught me to dance. He loved to Jitterbug, Swing, and Charleston.

"Wait!" my friend said, "That's six or seven

things."

My reply, "No, it's really only one. My Dad taught me that a personal relationship with God is the most important relationship I can have. Through that relationship, all of life is worship, for we were created to glorify God in and through everything! And, in grateful response to Him, we are to share the gospel with unbelievers and Christ-followers alike!

Then I realized why my friend asked me that question. He wanted me to focus on the wonderful things that my Dad taught me so that I would realize all things for which I should be thankful.

We are to give thanks in every circumstance in which we find ourselves. We should strive to be cognizant of all the amazing blessings the Lord has given us in our past and present and give Him thanks!

Prayer: My gracious Heavenly Father, I thank you for being my Abba Father, and for the gift of my earthly Dad who pointed me to You. In Jesus' name, Amen.

Thought for the Day: Remembering God's

blessings leads you to giving thanks to Him for those blessings.

Shop 'til You Drop

by Shirley
Read: 1 Timothy 6:6-10

But godliness with contentment is great gain.
1 Timothy 6:6 (NIV)

The day after Thanksgiving has come to be called Black Friday, one of the biggest shopping days of the year. It kicks off the Christmas shopping season. Stores open their doors early, close them late, or even stay open all night in hopes that their heavily marked-down prices will bring in many customers. This experience did not actually happen on Black Friday, but its lesson is very appropriate for that day and every day of the year.

As I was putting gasoline in my car one Saturday morning after Christmas, I overhead a little seven-year-old or eight-year-old boy talking to his dad who was putting gasoline in their van. The boy was explaining to his dad that he needed to buy a particular remote-control vehicle he wanted.

Dad said, "You already got a remote-control airplane, Jeep, and Corvette. You don't need another remote-control vehicle."

"Daddy, those aren't the ones I need. I need

this other car," replied the boy.

"You have three new remote-control vehicles. You will not get a fourth!"

"I never get anything I need!" argued the boy.

His dad replied, "So, you don't want the remote-control airplane, Jeep and Corvette, and the ...." and he listed about 15 other items the boy had apparently received as Christmas presents.

Suddenly, the little boy's whole demeanor and facial expression changed as the realization of where this conversation might be going hit him. "Yes, I want all of them, and, I need this other one, too!"

The dad calmly suggested, "Okay, let's return everything you said you wanted and get you what you really need."

The little boy sat on the pavement, with his hands cupping his chin and cried out, "You tricked me, Daddy!"

Dad lovingly said, "No, I didn't trick you. I just want you to realize that you have everything you need, and many, many other things you want. You told your mom and me and your grandparents what you wanted for Christmas, but now you want more because your friend has this other toy, and you suddenly have decided that you need one, too."

Then, the Dad reached down and scooped the little boy up in his arms. "Son, I want you to learn to be grateful for what you have and not to always be wanting more. And, I want you to learn the difference between wanting something and needing something."

You guessed it. This scene once again provided the Holy Spirit the opportunity to convict me! Too often, I am ungrateful for the people the Lord has brought into my life and the things the Lord has provided me. Like the little boy, I seem to want more and more and more, and I continually redefine my wants as needs in order to justify getting what I want.

I had a teary-eyed time on my drive to my destination that day as I confessed and repented to the Lord for my ungratefulness. Then, I spent time thanking the Lord for the people and things He has given me.

During this Thanksgiving week, let's remember to be truly thankful.

Prayer: Lord, teach me to be satisfied with the gifts You have given me, and give me a passion to know

You and want more, and more, and more of You! In Jesus' name, Amen.

Thought for the Day: I once read this quote: "We are a nation who tramples over each other in an effort to get more stuff one day after thanking God for what we have." Are we really thankful for what the Lord has given us?

Chapter 5: 'Tis the Season

Winter Joy

by Harriet
Read: James 1:1-4

*Consider it all joy, my brethren, when you
encounter various trials, knowing that the
testing of faith produces endurance.*
James 1:2-3 (NASB)

Yum! I pulled a freshly baked apple pie from
the oven, and the heavenly aroma filled my kitchen
wafting its way through the house. I set it down on
the countertop near the oven to cool. I had spent the
prior hour chopping fresh apples my family had
picked at a local farm. The crust was baked to a
perfect golden brown, crystals of sugar glistened on
the top. My children gathered in the kitchen, one by
one, excited for the pie to cool. The smell of
cinnamon and apples made their little mouths water
as they begged me to let them have some … before
dinner!

I succumbed to their pleas. After all, dinner
was still at least an hour away. Hopefully my
children would have their appetites back by then.
How often do they have a chance to eat a piece of
pie straight out of the oven anyway? As I cut the
pie, one of the children asked if it had been made

from the apples they had picked a week earlier at a local farm. What a great opportunity to teach my children a life lesson.

"Did you know that apple trees need cold weather in order to produce yummy apples like the ones in this pie?"

I asked them as I gave each a slice—but a small one so as not to ruin their dinner. "It is true." I explained further. "Most hardy fruit trees need a certain amount of cold winter weather before they can end their dormancy to promote spring growth."

When winters are too mild, spring growth is delayed, irregular and slow. The period of blooming is extended late into the spring so the possibility of frost injury is increased. If our winter the year before had been too mild, my family would not have been able to enjoy the delicious apple pie they would soon be happily nibbling in spite of their upcoming dinner.

Then I explained to my children that in many ways people are like the fruit trees. We too need some winter in our lives—some challenging and even difficult days. For it is through difficulties that we grow. The challenges we face today will produce fruit in our lives tomorrow.

That is one reason passages like today's key verse are so powerful. This verse in James says we should consider it joy when we face trials because it will produce endurance.

Next time you are facing trials and tribulations in your life, think of the fruit trees and the delicious pies you may be able to enjoy because these trees saw some cold days. Thank God for what He is producing in your life. And too, as the cold winter winds blow in this year, think of the yummy fruit that you will be able to eat next year because of the cold the trees endured in order to produce that fruit.

Prayer: Heavenly Father, be with us when we face trials and troubles. Help us to learn to count it all as joy. And thank You for the fruit You are producing in our lives. In Your Son's name, Amen.

Thought for the Day: Without cold winter days, there would be no summer fruit. Without difficult days, we would not grow spiritually and emotionally. Count it all joy!

Plain Ole Folks

by Shirley
Read: Luke 2:8-16

And there were shepherds living out in the fields
nearby, keeping watch over their flocks at night.
An angel of the Lord appeared to them,
and the glory of the Lord shone around them,
and they were terrified.
Luke 2:8-9 (NIV)

Have you ever thought what it must have been like for the shepherds in the field when the angel appeared to them?

"Fear not!" proclaimed the angel.

"Easy for you to say!" would likely have been my reaction had I been a shepherd that night. The angel continued with the announcement that Jesus, the Savior of the world, had been born, thus fulfilling numerous Old Testament prophecies concerning the promised Savior.

Seeing one angel would have been frightening enough, but can you imagine your response to what happened next?

> "And suddenly there was with the
> angel a multitude of the heavenly
> host praising God and saying,

'Glory to God in the highest, and
on earth peace, goodwill toward
men'" (Luke 2:13-14 NKJV).

Really, God? You send an angel and a
heavenly host to a bunch of plain ole shepherds in
the dark of the night to tell them to go seek the
Savior of the world?

Picture the scene. The shepherds were tending
their sheep that night just as they always had, when
suddenly, a glorious light blazed into and dispelled
the darkness with a brightness these lowly
shepherds had never seen. Then an angel spoke
directly to them, proclaiming a message that had
not been heard since the days of the prophets.

This extravagant announcement of the King of
kings' birth was not delivered to dignitaries or
rulers, nor to Pharisees, or priests. Instead, it came
at midnight to a group of lowly shepherds who were
hard at work tending their sheep.

Have you ever wondered why God announced
His Son in this manner? After all, God was
announcing not only the birth of His Son, but also
the arrival of the one through whom salvation
would come. James 2:5 gives us a hint. It says, "Has
not God chosen those who are poor in the eyes of

the world to be rich in faith and to inherit the kingdom He promised to those who love Him?"

Moses was trying to hide, David was keeping his sheep, Elisha was plowing, Paul was intent on slaughtering the disciples, and Peter and Andrew were fishing when God burst into their lives. And yes, God even burst into the lives of a handful of ragged men who were tending their sheep. These men were changed forever when the angel and heavenly host, surrounded by God's glory, appeared and proclaimed, "Glory to God in the highest heaven, and on earth peace to those on whom his favor rests!"

In the way that shepherds care for and seek out their lost sheep, we get a glimpse of how God came to seek, to save, and to care for those who are lost (Luke 19:10). I am so grateful to the Lord for loving us sinful, plain ole folks enough to seek us out when we are dead in our trespasses and sin. He took upon Himself the punishment for our sin that we deserve, and, by His grace, made us alive together with Christ (Ephesians 2:1-10). Soli Deo Gloria! (For the Glory of God Alone!)

Prayer: Heavenly Father, You rule over all things.

Yet, You announced the birth of the Savior to lowly shepherds. You care about even plain ole folks like me. Thank You for loving me and desiring a relationship with me. In Your Son's name, Amen.

Thought for the Day: Jesus came to earth to seek and to save those who are lost, even me.

The Still, Small Voice

by Harriet

Read: 1 Kings 19:11-13, John 10:27

And after the earthquake a fire;
but the Lord was not in the fire:
and after the fire a still small voice.
1 Kings 19:12 (NKJV)

I will always remember that Christmas morning. Someone in my family recalls the events of that morning nearly every Christmas, causing the rest of us to chuckle at the memory. I was eleven or twelve years old, and my family was back in the States experiencing a typical American Christmas full of snowy weather, warm houses, and store-bought gifts. Christmas had been all we could have hoped for that year, and my contented family sat around the table eating a delicious Christmas breakfast of sausage, eggs, fruit, biscuits, coffee, and orange juice.

The happy chatter of Christmas breakfast was abruptly interrupted by my younger sister, Marianne.

"Pass me the butter!" she screamed.

My mother reacted swiftly. Such behavior would simply not be tolerated. "Young lady, we do not raise our voices at the dinner table like that!" Mother spoke in her most authoritative tone. Then, after this sharp correction of the rude behavior, Marianne was sent to her room.

Marianne was the youngest of my parents' four children. She was a quiet child with a winsome personality, always a pleasure to be around. Outbursts like this were unheard of from her and completely out of character. Everyone at the table was shocked. With her upstairs pouting in her room, the rest of the family began discussing what had come over her that she should behave so rudely. She was all of about eight years old at the time.

Well, it just so happened that my older brother had received a tape recorder as a Christmas gift just hours earlier, and in his eagerness to try out his new toy, he had recorded the table conversation that morning. "I've been trying out my new gift and recording things all morning. Let's see if we can figure out why Marianne got so angry."

He played the recording back. As we listened, we heard the clatter of dishes as people passed them around, the almost constant chatter of family members talking; we had a large family of six, after all. And occasionally, throughout the recording, we heard Marianne's small voice saying, "Could you pass the butter please?" "Please pass the butter." "I need some butter; would someone pass it to me please?" Her unheeded requests grew louder and louder, until finally she exploded with her outburst of, "Pass me the butter!"

None of us had heard my little sister's small, quiet voice asking for someone to pass her the butter. And as she waited, her biscuit grew colder and colder, even as her request grew louder and louder.

According to this passage in 1 Kings, God sometimes speaks in a small voice. The rest of my family and I were too preoccupied with our own concerns to hear my sister's small voice. Are we likewise sometimes too preoccupied with our lives to hear God's voice? Spending time in God's word, to read for ourselves what He is saying, helps us focus on Him so that we will not get preoccupied with all the other things that vie for our attention during the holiday season.

I am reminded of words to an old hymn, "Open, Lord, My Inward Ear," by Charles Wesley, who wrote:

"Open, Lord, my inward ear,
And bid my heart rejoice;
Bid my quiet spirit hear
The comfort of Thy voice:

Never in the whirlwind found,
Or where earthquakes rock the place,
Still and silent is the sound,
The whisper, of Thy grace."

Prayer: Heavenly Father, tune our ears to hear Your voice. In Your Son's name, Amen.

Thought for the Day: God's sheep hear His voice and they follow Him. Listen for God's voice today.

Christmas Catastrophes

by Harriet
Read: Ecclesiastes 3:11-13

*After they had heard the king,
they went on their way,
and the star they had seen when it rose
went ahead of them until it stopped
over the place where the child was.
Matthew 2:9 (NIV)*

It felt more like summer than Christmastime. The crowd gathered on the back lawn of Frances Jones—a missionary guest house named for a former missionary who had lost her life to yellow fever in this tropical country I called home. I was a child in the audience, too young to make the cast. My sister was an angel. She and a few others, dressed in white sheets with cloth covered wire wings and halos, stood ready to sing when given their queue. My brother was one of the wise men who would be singing "We Three Kings." I was excited for them ... but mostly; I was just excited!

On the far end of the lawn stood a stable that would soon house Mary, Joseph, and baby Jesus. This year baby Jesus was only a doll, instead of a real baby like some years. Next to the stable, sheep grazed with a group of little shepherds nearby trying to maintain control. These always made the play interesting. The little actors took their roles quite seriously trying to stay composed, no matter what.

Usually, a large cardboard star covered in tinfoil rested on top of the stable, but this year was special! This year, one of the missionaries attached a rope to the roof of the stable and extended it across the lawn to the roof of Frances Jones. The star was to be illuminated from the ground while it was pulled across the lawn on this rope in front of the wise men as they walked toward the stable. What a great play it was going to be! How proud I was to have my brother walking under that spotlighted star!

The play started without a hitch. The narrator read the Christmas story from the book of Luke, "It came to pass in those days ...." As he spoke, the young actors playing Mary and Joseph slowly made their way to the stable.

Between the stable and the shepherds, my sister and the other angels, were elevated on a table that had been draped with a white cloth. These were the heavenly hosts standing on clouds, singing to the shepherds. However, owing to the fact that the heavenly hosts had no microphones, their song was difficult to hear. The little shepherds alternated between chasing lost sheep and shouting in loud stage whispers, "Louder! Louder!"

But the show must go on. Soon the wise men made their entrance. My brother and his cohorts began their trek from the corner of the guest house toward the stable following the lighted star and singing as they went. "… O star of wonder, star of night, star with royal beauty bright …."

Midway to the stable, catastrophe struck! The rope broke and the star of wonder went crashing to the ground. Undeterred, the wise men continued on, each stepping over the fallen star as they came upon it, still singing its accolades and looking upward as if it were still in front of them.

God's word tells us that God makes everything beautiful in its time—even errant sheep and fallen stars. This Christmas as cakes fall, gifts you want to purchase are sold out, loved ones get stuck in traffic and do not arrive on time, and other catastrophes happen, guard the peace of the season in your heart. It will someday be a cherished memory.

Prayer: Heavenly Father, as You work to make everything beautiful, help us to praise You even in our imperfections. In Your precious Son's name, Amen.

Thought for the Day: God loves us, flaws and all!

Ganma, I Don't Need a Tree!

by Shirley
Read: Ephesians 1:1-9

*Little children, let us not love in word or talk
but in deed and in truth.*
1 John 3:18

While waiting at the pharmacy to pick up some allergy medicine, I overheard an interesting conversation between a woman and a little boy whom I had heard tell someone he was "almost eight years old!" The little boy told his grandmother that she should tell his dad to get him a Christmas tree and decorate it today!

"I don't have a tree either. So, it's okay that you don't have one yet," replied the elderly woman. That caught my attention, so I lingered in the aisle picking up and flipping through a *Popular Mechanics* magazine just so I could watch and hear this exchange.

"Why?" asked the little boy.

With a slight hint of disappointment in her voice, the woman said, "I have to buy groceries, so no tree."

"But you need a tree and I do, too!" replied the boy.

The grandmother stooped down eye-to-eye with the little boy and asked, "Why do I need a Christmas tree when I have you to decorate my life?"

The little boy did something that I did not expect. He gave his grandmother a huge hug and said, "Ganma, I don't need a tree!"

You guessed it! Ganma, the couple of other women in earshot, and I were all in tears. Now I really was intrigued!

The little boy grabbed hold of his Ganma's hand and said, "Look at this!" as he pulled three pennies from his pocket. "Ganma, can you get a tree with this?" He put the pennies in her hand.

"Yes darlin', let's go get Ganma a little tree as soon as I get my medicine," Ganma said, apparently giving in to her grandson's desire for her to have a tree.

In the meantime, behind Ganma, I saw a man walk up to the pharmacist, pull out his wallet, and hand the pharmacist two twenty-dollar bills as he motioned to the woman. Ganma went up to get her medication and handed the pharmacist her money. When he returned her change, he handed her the forty dollars and mouthed, "For your tree."

Ganma just stood there for a minute. As she turned around I saw a little tear running down her cheek as she took the little boy's hand and left the pharmacy. That little boy walked out with his head held high. I heard him say, "Ganma, I'm glad you are getting a Christmas tree!"

I wish I knew the whole story. Nothing that was said or done gave any indication that Ganma was or was not a Christ-follower. I wonder what made that little boy go from demanding that Ganma and he have a tree, to giving Ganma his only three pennies so she could have a tree. What accounted for his change from selfish desire to generosity?

Whatever their situation, the Lord used this experience to convict me of my own selfishness and lack of generosity. God is so generous to us as He lavishes His grace, mercy, and love upon us, isn't He? We celebrate God's generous gift of His Son who came to earth as a baby and who, as fully God and fully man, hung on the cross, died, rose from the grave, and redeemed us forever!

Prayer: Gracious Heavenly Father, You lavish good gifts upon Your children. May we be mindful of all Your blessings at this time of year when we

celebrate Your greatest blessing—the gift of Jesus!
In whose name we pray, Amen.

Thought for the Day: What a great love God
lavishes upon us!

Chapter 6: Keeping Christ in Christmas

Joy to the World!

by Shirley
Read: Psalm 96:1-3, Psalm 98:1-6

*I will give thanks to the Lord
because of his righteousness;
I will sing the praises of the name
of the Lord Most High.
Psalm 7:17 (NIV)*

I looked into the rearview mirror as I was stopped at a traffic light. The lady in the car behind me was smiling and singing at the top of her lungs. I couldn't tell what she was singing. The light changed and, as we continued a little way down the road, I promptly forgot about this lady and her singing.

A couple of minutes later, I turned into the parking lot of the grocery store and tried to find a parking space that wouldn't require a 5k walk to get into the store. I found a parking place, got out of my car, and walked toward the store. Just then I saw the singing lady pull into a parking spot a couple of aisles over. She was still smiling and singing at the top of her lungs! By now she had my curiosity up, and I had to know what she was singing.

I took a little tour of the parking lot so I could

walk by her car, just to see if I could tell what she was singing. A security officer who saw me walk from one aisle to the next stopped and asked if I needed help finding my car! (Thankfully, not this time!)

As I got closer to her car I heard the music playing loudly on her radio. She had opened her door just a little bit as she majestically, albeit off-key, belted out the last verse of the Christmas carol "Joy to the World."

"He rules the world, with truth and grace;
and makes the nations prove,
the glories of His righteousness;
and wonders of His love,
and wonders of His love,
and wonders and wonders of His love!"

As I passed the back of her car, she turned off her engine, climbed out of the car, and repeated loudly and deliberately, "And wonders, and wonders of His love!"

At that point, she turned and noticed me looking at her and said, "I can't sing, but I'm trying to make a joyful noise!"

I smiled back at the lady and responded by telling her that, to God's ears, she was indeed making a joyful noise unto Him, and that the Bible tells us to make a loud noise, rejoice, and sing praises to Him.

In my mother's latter years, when her voice was not as good as it had once been, Mom would say, "I can't carry a tune in a bucket, but I can make a joyful noise!" This, like the lady's comment, was, of course, a reference to Psalm 98:4.

The lady walked toward the store singing, "O Come, All Ye Faithful." How wonderful that this lady who could barely carry a tune was praising her Lord and Savior with reckless abandon! Yet again, I was convicted of my lack of boldness to praise Him anywhere and everywhere. With the hectic pace of the holiday, I pray that we will not forget that the due response to God's gift to us—His Son, eternal life—is praise!

Prayer: Lord, we praise You! And we thank You for all You have done for us. You gave us life and then gave us eternal life through Your Son. At this busy time of the year, when we think of gift giving, may we not forget to offer you the gift of praise. In Jesus' name, Amen.

Thought for the Day: With what songs of praise is your heart filled?

The Box

by Harriet
Read: Colossians 1:9-12

For this reason, since the day we heard about you,
we have not stopped praying for you.
We continually ask God to fill you with the
knowledge of his will through all the wisdom and
understanding that the Spirit gives.
Colossians 1:9 (NIV)

While wrapping Christmas presents a few years back, I chose a small box that looked to be the perfect size for a gift card. Now that my children are grown, I sometimes like to buy and give them gift cards to one of their favorite stores or restaurants, but I still prefer to wrap the gift cards, so they look like a small present in order to keep the suspense of the gift going until it's opened. That year, when I lifted the top of the box I had selected to put the gift card in, it already had a gift card in it. The card was to one of my sons, but it surprised me to see it because I thought I had already wrapped that card and put it under the tree.

So, I ran to the tree. Sure enough; there was the gift to my son that I thought contained this gift card resting under the tree alongside other gifts. It was a small box neatly wrapped in bright green metallic Christmas paper tied with silver ribbon and a silver bow. It was such a pretty looking Christmas gift sitting there under the tree. But apparently it did not contain the card I thought it did. I was perplexed.

"What is in this box?" I wondered out loud. I tried to remember what other small gifts or gift cards I had bought this particular son, but my mind was a complete blank. Perhaps I had accidently wrapped someone else's gift and labeled it for my son. Or maybe I had simply forgotten what I had purchased him, in spite of my attempts to record my various purchases, for just these kinds of reasons. I decided I had no choice but to open the box and view its contents.

Guess what was in the box? Absolutely nothing! The box was completely empty! Oh, how I laughed at myself for wrapping a completely empty box by mistake!

Are we like that sometimes? Do we look like we have it all together on the outside, but inside we are empty? Are we a very attractive package with nothing to anchor us inside? Have you known people like that? We live in an age where we are overly focused and concerned with our physical package. If we wanted to, we could spend a small fortune on items and ways to make our bodies more attractive—everything from clothing and make-up to put on them to procedures to do to them that will alter them for the better according to the current culture's way of thinking.

Of course, it is not wrong to try and present our best. We are representing God to an unbelieving world, after all. But are we at least as concerned with what is on the inside of us—what is in our hearts and minds—as we are our outward, physical appearance?

In today's passage, the Apostle Paul tells the believers at Colossae that he is praying for them to be filled with the knowledge of God's will through the Holy Spirit. And, he tells us what it looks like when we are filled with the Holy Spirit as he explains that this Spirit will give us the wisdom, understanding, and the knowledge of His will so that we can live a life that is worthy of God and that pleases Him.

Prayer: Fill us up, O Lord! Fill us with your Spirit and the knowledge of Your will so that we may walk in a manor worthy of You. In your Son's name, Amen.

Thought for the Day: Are you empty inside? God wants to fill you with His Spirit and make you beautiful on the inside, too.

Out of the Mouths of Babes

by Shirley
Read: Isaiah 11:1-6

"Do you hear what these children are saying?"
they asked him. "Yes," replied Jesus,
"have you never read,
'from the lips of children and infants you,
Lord, have called forth your praise?'"
Matthew 21:16 (NIV)

I love going to the bookstore and browsing through all the books. At Christmastime a few years ago, I stopped in the children's section to look at Christmas books. Even though I love reading and seeing the vivid colors and depictions in children's books, I was on a mission to help a friend find a specific book that her granddaughter wanted.

There was a little girl, who looked to be about seven or eight, sitting on the floor with a huge picture storybook about Christmas in her lap. Beside her was her toddler brother who did not appear very happy to be sitting down. The sister was animatedly reading the story to her little brother. From time to time she asked him if he was listening. He wasn't.

As I drew closer to the children, I realized that

the little girl was not actually reading the book. She was telling her brother about each picture in the book. I moved around behind the children, and I could see that the pages of the book were filled with vividly colored drawings of Christmas-related items: decorated trees, snowmen, reindeer, wrapped presents, and other such things. As the little girl turned the pages she would identify the items in the picture and tell her brother how each one related to Christmas.

"This is a Christmas tree. You put pretty lights and things on it and make it look beautiful." She then turned the page and said, "This is a snowman. We don't have snowmen. But it's a snowman anyway." She turned another page. "This is a Christmas present. I think it's a baby doll."

That was the last picture in the book, which seemed to disturb the little girl, and she got fairly agitated. A lady, whom I soon determined was the little girl's aunt, came over and sat beside her and asked what was wrong.

The little girl cried, "I don't like this book! It doesn't have Jesus!"

The aunt had a confused look on her face. "What?"

The little girl said, "Jesus is not in this book. Why?"

The aunt seemed to be struggling to find an answer. Finally, she said, "It isn't a book about Jesus, it's a book about Christmas!"

Of course, I found myself thinking, "Excuse me? Christmas isn't about Jesus Christ?"

Meanwhile, the little girl looked straight into her aunt's eyes and said boldly, "But my daddy told me Christmas *is* about Jesus!"

The aunt abruptly dismissed the subject by saying "We have to go."

I said a silent prayer thanking God for this little girl's daddy who told her that Christmas is about Jesus. And I prayed for this aunt who may not really understand what Christmas is, and more importantly, who Christ is.

Let's make certain that we do not get so involved with all the decorations and trimmings of Christmas that we leave Christ out of our story of Christmas, for without Christ there is no Christmas.

Prayer: Gracious Heavenly Father, thank You for parents who love and serve You by teaching their children about You. Help us to keep Christ central in our celebration of Christmas. In Jesus' name, Amen.

Thought for the Day: Your children are never too young for you to teach them about who Jesus Christ is and that He is the center of our Christmas celebration.

The Day is Near

by Harriet
Read: Romans 13:11-12

For now we see in a mirror dimly,
but then face to face.
1 Corinthians 13:12a)

Have you ever considered the fact that at the first advent, those waiting did not know for whom they waited? Oh, they knew some things about Him, but they did not know who He was going to be really—what He would look like, or even to what family He would belong. They knew from Scripture He would be a descendant of King David, but which descendant? Who were His mother and father going to be? And when would He come?

Of course, the prophets of old had given them some indications of what He would be like. At best, those prophecies must have been confusing to the people. The prophecies said that He was to be a child born of a woman, a virgin in fact, in the town of Bethlehem (Isaiah 6:9, Genesis 3:15, Micah 5:2, Isaiah 7:14). But at the same time, He was also to be the Son of God (Psalm 2:7). To add to the confusion, He would be forsaken by God (Psalm 22:1), but also seated at the right hand of God

(Psalm 110:1). He would be a man of sorrows, crushed for our sins (Isaiah 53:3-12), and yet also a king (Zechariah 9:9).

How could the people at that time make sense of all of that? That is where faith came in to play. Although they did not understand, the people waited in faith for their Messiah. But they waited for a stranger. At that time, they knew and worshipped a God whose voice was too terrible to behold and whose face too awesome to see. Remember, Moses was told if he looked at God's face, he would die.

Our waiting season is different. In this Christmas season, we celebrate the birth of a Savior whom we know. He is a Savior whose face is glorious, according to 2 Corinthians 4:6, and whose voice is tender.

In today's passage, Paul tells us that we should understand the times, for our salvation is near. Paul also says night is nearly over, and the day is almost here. Is your salvation near? Do you know Jesus as your personal Savior? Have you had that moment in your life when you realized your need for a Savior?

I remember the day I accepted Jesus as my

Savior. I was a child in Vacation Bible School at the annual meeting of the mission in Nigeria; Mission Meeting as we called it. I walked down the aisle of the seminary chapel in Ogbomoso where our Bible school was held. Later my pastor, Rev. Ogunyele, came to my house to make sure I understood what I had done, and after that I was baptized in my local Nigerian church. I remember it well.

Do you have a moment in your life where you know you specifically accepted Jesus as your Savior? It is our prayer that you do, but if you do not, what better time to receive Jesus as your personal Savior than Christmas? This, then, is the joy of our advent.

Prayer: Heavenly Father, thank You for giving us Jesus—a Savior we can now know personally. In Jesus' name, Amen.

Thought for the Day: We now know what the men of old did not know, and someday we will know even more fully, even as we are also known.

Happy Birthday, Jesus!

by Shirley
Read: Galatians 4:4-7

But when the set time had fully come,
God sent his Son, born of a woman,
born under the law,
to redeem those under the law ....
Galatians 4:4-5a

My sister has a different kind of Christmas tradition. Every year, she bakes and decorates a birthday cake for Jesus. She includes her granddaughters who have so much fun preparing, baking, and decorating the cake. As our extended family gathers together, we all bring our specialty dish to add to our meal. We have a wonderful time of fellowship as we enjoy our feast. After everyone has consumed way too much of our delicious Christmas dinner, we light the candles on the birthday cake and sing "Happy Birthday" to Jesus. The children in the crowd—nieces, nephews, grandchildren, and even grown up children like me—join our voices in singing.

Once we have sung, the children blow out all of the birthday candles, and we get to enjoy the delicious birthday cake.

What a great reminder through something that is fairly commonplace in our lives—birthdays and birthday cakes. We all can remember the joy of celebrating birthdays as children. When I was a child in Nigeria, because so many missionaries were stationed in my town of Ogbomoso, there were quite a few other missionary kids to celebrate my birthday with me. It was a special time and a source of great memories.

Regardless of our age, we love celebrating our birthdays and hearing family and friends sing "Happy Birthday" to us, don't we? Reading birthday cards, receiving phone calls and presents, and friends gathering for a party make us feel special. We love it when people make a big deal of the fact that we were born. Many of us also enjoy spending copious amounts of time choosing just the right card and gift for our loved ones and planning a fun party to celebrate their birthday.

So why would we not give at least the same amount of thought and planning into celebrating Jesus' birthday at Christmas? Sometimes it appears that we are properly celebrating Jesus' birthday because of the way the inside and outside of our homes are so extravagantly decorated, and the tree has a gazillion beautifully wrapped packages under it. Yet, the presence of extravagant decorations and beautifully wrapped packages do not necessarily comprise a proper celebration of Jesus' birthday. Why not? Because oftentimes we do all of these things for ourselves, and not for God's glory.

What is often missing in our celebrations is intentional planning that makes Christmas a celebration of the birth of the King of kings and Lord of lords, our Savior Jesus Christ.

One way our family does this is by enjoying the birthday cake for Jesus, made by my sister and her granddaughters, as we sing and celebrate the fact that He was born. This year as you celebrate, focus on the truth of this passage in Galatians which tells us that at just the right time God sent His Son to redeem you and me! In the excitement and busyness of your day, remember to celebrate the birth of Christ on Christmas Day and every day of the year. Christ the Savior is born!

Prayer: Gracious Heavenly Father, we thank You for Your invitation to Your Son's birthday celebration. May we celebrate His birth in a worthy manner. In Jesus' name, Amen.

Thought for the Day: In the excitement and busyness of your day, remember to celebrate the birth of Christ every day of the year! Christ the Savior is born!

Chapter 7: It's Christmas!

For Unto Us a Child is Born

by Harriet
Read: Psalm 24:7-10

For unto us a child is born,
and unto us a Son is given,
and the government shall be on his shoulders.
And his name shall be called
Wonderful, Counselor,
Mighty God, Everlasting Father, Prince of Peace.
Isaiah 9:6 (KJV)

Have you ever waited for the birth of a child? Those last few weeks before the child arrives can sometimes seem to last an eternity. I have four children and two grandchildren, and all seemed to take forever to get here. And with every passing day, the anticipation of the coming birth increased. Will the baby be a boy or a girl? What colors will his or her eyes, hair, and even skin tone be? What will his or her facial features be like? Will he or she favor his father or his mother? Or, perhaps the baby will have recessive genes and look like great uncle or aunt so and so. Then finally, one day, that much anticipated moment arrives, and the unseen becomes seen. The precious little baby is delivered!

The Old Testament men and women of faith knew a Savior was coming. They waited for Him like a family waits for a baby to be born. They knew some things about the coming Savior but did not understand it all fully. Today's passage (Psalm 24:9 NASB) is a very familiar one.

> "Lift up your heads, O gates!
> And be lifted up, O ancient doors,
> that the King of glory may come in!"

But it quickly asks the question, "Who is the King of glory?" Then this passage offers an answer to that question—He is "the Lord, strong and mighty, the Lord mighty in battle." That is all true, of course. He conquered sin on the cross, and we see Him come again as the King He is in the book of Revelation. But, He came to this world as a tiny little baby, flesh and needy like any human baby that has ever been born.

My grandson was a preemie. Born six weeks early, he became septic shortly after birth. For two weeks, he lay in a bassinet in a neonatal intensive care unit, hooked up to intravenous fluids and monitors. Today he is a strong, healthy child. But once, he was tiny and fragile.

Our Savior is like that, strong and mighty, yes,

yet born to us as a precious little baby. When my mother was pregnant with her first child, my father would tell her, "Bring me home a bundle!" Well, God sent us a bundle that first Christmas morning so long ago.

Christmas is a season of anticipation. We anticipate the gifts we will receive. We anticipate the friends and family we will see, and the delicious foods we will eat. Today, it is a season full of traditions that we happily participate in as we anticipate the coming day. But, back in the Old Testament times, they did not have Christmas traditions. Yet, they did have the anticipation of the coming Savior. They were filled with questions and searched the scriptures trying to find the answers. What would He be like?

Today we know. He would be the King of glory, strong and mighty, but He would also be a child born to them … and to us.

Prayer: Heavenly Father, thank You for sending Your Son to us as a tiny, helpless baby. Thank You that He is also the King, strong and mighty. And, thank You that weak as we are, through Him we too are more than conquers. In Jesus's name, Amen.

Thought for the Day: The King of glory came to us as a helpless, little bundle of joy.

Her Perfect Christmas

by Shirley
Read: Psalm 145:4-7

This is love: not that we loved God,
but that he loved us
and sent his Son as an atoning sacrifice
for our sins.
1 John 4:10 (NKJV)

On Christmas Eve a few years ago, I observed a very sad scene in the grocery store. A woman had an emotional meltdown as she screamed at the store manager, blaming him for ruining her Christmas because the store did not carry the brand of eggnog she needed for her Christmas dinner. Nothing the manager said helped the situation. In fact, with every word the manager spoke, the woman's anger increased.

I noticed a teenage girl a few aisles over from me watching the scene with a look of absolute horror on her face. Then, my heart broke as huge crocodile tears began streaming down her face, and she began sobbing as she sank to the floor. I walked over to ask the girl if there was anything I could do to help.

Pointing to the lady she said, "No! She makes

all of us miserable trying to recreate the impossible—her perfect Christmas from forty years ago!"

Many of us have a picture in our minds of what our perfect Christmas looks like. Sometimes that picture is based on a wonderful Christmas we remember from our past. And oftentimes, that picture is created as the polar opposite of a horrible Christmas that still haunts us. In order to create that perfect Christmas, we spend copious amounts of time decorating our homes, running from store to store purchasing all the gifts that are just right for all the people on our gift list, staying up late to wrap each gift in just the right color paper and ribbon, and gathering all the ingredients needed to make everyone's favorite dish for Christmas dinner. Before Christmas Day ever arrives, we are absolutely exhausted!

We do a great job convincing ourselves that we are making Christmas about our families and what they want, yet we are really just busy making Christmas all about us and what we want. Nothing about our thoughts, attitudes, facial expressions, or words exhibit an ounce of gratefulness and joy that Christ, our Savior, is born.

Then, if on Christmas Day the gift opening, dinner, whatever it is, does not match the perfect picture of Christmas that we have in our minds, we plummet into a deep depression, get angry with and blame everyone around us as we make ourselves and everyone else miserable!

Our attempts at recreating that perfect Christmas are often attempts to regain a feeling of love, worth, and security that we felt during that wonderful Christmas in our past.

However, recreating an event from the past will never be as perfect as one's memory of that event. Nor will it provide us the feelings of love, worth, and security for which we long. Instead of trying to recreate something that will never be as perfect as we remember, choose instead to celebrate the birth of Jesus Christ our Savior and Lord, who is love, and the reason we have worth and security. Create new traditions and memories that you, your family, and everyone around you will enjoy for years to come!

Prayer: Heavenly Father, help us recognize that in You alone will we find love, worth, and security. In Jesus' name, Amen.

Thought for the Day: Take time this Christmas to refocus your heart on the "Savior, who is Christ the Lord!"

God's Gift of Love

by: Harriet
Read: John 3:16-18, 1 John 4:8

For God so loved the world that He gave
His only begotten Son,
that whoever believes in Him
should not perish, but have eternal life.
John 3:16 (NASB)

What does love look like? If someone asked you to describe love, how would you describe it? What words would you choose to express your understanding of love? Would you speak of the love between a man and a woman? Or would you tell of love for others—love of family, perhaps, or one's fellow man? If someone asked you to draw a picture of love, what would you draw?

Ask a child to draw love, and he might draw a heart. Yes, surely a bright red or pink heart has come to symbolize love; sometimes it has an arrow through it. We see this symbol all over the place on cards or decorations that celebrate love. Actually, the heart and arrow come from a Greek myth about a little child-like god named Cupid who was supposed to have been the son of Venus, the goddess of love. According to the myth, Cupid lurked around carrying a bow and arrows. If he shot one of his arrows through a person's heart, then that person would fall in love immediately. Aside from not being true, does a big colorful heart or a story of a little boy-god shooting arrows really convey the essence of love?

No. The Bible shows us a very different picture of love. According to the Scripture love looks like a baby in a manger—approximately seven pounds of helpless flesh, sleeping contentedly or perhaps crying in hunger just like any other baby. But this baby was not in a warm, clean crib in a brightly painted room; no, this baby was in a stable full of dirty animals because there was no bed for Him among humans. And this mother had no pretty crocheted or flannel blue blankets for her child, so she bundled him in the only thing she had—long strips of cloth, which she wrapped around Him to swaddle Him and keep Him warm.

In the Bible, love also looks like a young man in the prime of life bleeding and dying on a cross. It looks like this man willingly giving up His life so that others might gain theirs. Love looks like the everlasting God, in all His glory, becoming flesh and hanging on a cross. And it also looks like this same man as a baby wrapped in swaddling clothes and lying in a manger.

At this special season, let us recall the rawness of God's love story. This, God's plan for redeeming His creation, is filled with human tenderness, human trials, and human pain. This story is as real as love gets.

Prayer: Loving Father, Your love story is the truest form of love. Thank You for sending Your Son to die for me and all who will accept Your gift of salvation. Help us to remember Your great love for us during this Christmas season. In His name, Amen.

Thought for the Day: God is love!

In-laws, Out-laws, and
Strays off the Street

by Shirley
Read: Luke 14:21b-23, Hebrews 13:1-2

Be joyful at your festival—you,
your sons and daughters,
your male and female servants, and the Levites,
the foreigners, the fatherless and the widows
who live in your towns.
Deuteronomy 16:14 (NASB)

Every year as I sort through boxes of Christmas decorations, many precious memories flood my mind. I fondly remember the Christmas that Mom, my brother Tim, and I invited seemingly everyone we knew to our home for Christmas dinner. We invited family, in-laws, out-laws, and even strays off the street to join us.

We had a huge celebration at our home that year. There were six decorated trees inside, each one with different themes. One tree was decorated with elegant Victorian-style ornaments of lace, feathers, crystal, gold filigree, and silk with tiny pastel-colored twinkling lights and a beautiful gold-filigree angel on top. One tree had red, green, and red/green plaid ornaments with large lights that were also red and green. Another was decorated with old-fashioned and hand-made ornaments of all kinds and colors.

A vintage silver tree with blue ornaments reminded us of one we had in Nigeria, with a multi-colored light wheel shining on the tree that made the silver needles glow with the changing colors of the wheel. Mom had a small tree in her room that was decorated with tiny multi-colored blinking lights and beautifully colored crystal hummingbirds and butterflies. We also had a tree decorated with religious ornaments, such as crosses, angels, and nativity scene figurines. That tree had a cross on the top. There were also several more trees outdoors on the front porch, in the front and side yards, lining the driveway and across the road by the mailbox. Everything was decorated to the hilt.

Now, anyone who knew Tim knew how much he loved our mother and how much he loved making everything just right for *his* mom. That year, Tim and I worked all day and night Christmas Eve and until about three o'clock Christmas morning. We inspected each room from every possible angle to make certain everything was perfectly placed and decorated. There was not a nook nor cranny left undecorated. We had such a good time getting several little surprises ready for Mom to find later in the morning. We even planned to cook and serve Mom breakfast in bed, but she beat us into the kitchen because she had to make her dressing for later in the day.

I cannot remember how many people came for dinner that day, but the house was full of family, friends, and strays off the street. Mom would fuss at me when I would use the phrase "strays off the street" saying, "They are not unwanted strays, they are our new friends." And in fact, as the years rolled on, so many of those strays off the street became dear friends with whom I am still in contact.

That Christmas our home was also full of laughter, story-telling, and sweet tear-shared memories as one of my uncles read the Luke 2 account of the birth of Jesus, another uncle read a favorite Christmas poem, we sang Christmas carols, and prayed together.

What we did not know then, and what I remember now with fresh tears, is that it was our last Christmas with Tim, who passed away suddenly the following summer.

How grateful I am for the wonderful memories of that and many other Christmases I have known in my lifetime both here in the States and in Nigeria during my childhood. What always made Christmas wonderful was celebrating the birth of Jesus with family, friends, and yes, even strays off the street!

Prayer: Thank You Father for sending Your Son to be the Savior of the world, and more specifically, to be my Savior. In His name, Amen.

Thought for the Day: As you celebrate the birth of your Savior this year, remember to include those who may be alone during this season.

The Person of Christmas
by Shirley
Read: Romans 7:1-7

*... fixing our eyes on Jesus, the author
and perfecter of faith ....*
Hebrews 12:2 (NASB)

"You cannot extract the principles of Christmas from the Person of Christmas."

My pastor friend reminded me of this quote, whose source I do not know, one Sunday morning during the Christmas season. While this quote is true, we still see all around us the world's feeble attempts to extract the principles of Christmas from the Person of Christmas. We see it in movies, television shows, advertisements, songs, and greeting cards, don't we? We pull out the principles of peace on earth, love, joy, unity, and mercy and focus on them as if they all stand in a vast vacuum totally unrelated to Jesus Christ, the Person of Christmas.

The Santa Claus character that is now so symbolic of Christmas has morphed into a person who possesses the characteristics and power that, in fact, belong to Jesus Christ alone. Spend a little time watching some of the many Christmas movies on television, and you will see that the primary focus is on love for and peace with each other. We are also led to believe that all of this love and peace is the result of the goodness of a person's heart. Sometimes the main character's good heart has been buried deep by the pain, anger, and bitterness of a past event or a series of events. And, through another series of gut-wrenching circumstances, by the end of the story the goodness in the character's heart resurfaces as he or she unites or reunites in love and peace with everyone. The bottom-line message is to follow your heart and good things will happen to you and those you love.

What is wrong with that?

There is one gigantic oversight: the story is devoid of Jesus Christ! While these traits are certainly manifestations of some of the principles of Christmas, the love and peace of Christmas are primarily about the Person of Christmas, Jesus Christ. Christmas is about the love of God for us, and the focus of the peace is our peace with God. That is why God sent Jesus—because God loves us and wants us to have peace with Him, a peace which is only possible through Jesus, the Person of Christmas.

We are not to follow our hearts, we are to follow Jesus Christ and allow the Holy Spirit-inspired Word to guide us as we love and live in peace with each other.

As you think of all the many joys the Christmas season brings, do not forget to celebrate the Person of Christmas, Jesus Christ, as you celebrate the principles of Christmas. Today's key verse reminds us to fix our eyes on Jesus, the author and perfecter of our faith—the real reason for the Christmas season. He is also the author and perfecter of the peace and love of which this season is so full. As the words of the well-known Christmas carol say, "O come, let us adore Him, Christ the Lord!" He is the Person of Christmas in whom the principles of Christmas originate and live!

Prayer: Gracious Heavenly Father, thank You for loving us enough to give us the gift of Your Son Jesus Christ, for without His birth, our rebirth as Your children would not have been possible. Help us to not extract the principles of Christmas from the Person of Christmas. In Jesus' name, Amen.

Thought for the Day: Remember during this busy time of the year that your relationship with the Person of Christmas is your top priority. Spend time in His word and in prayer throughout your day.

Chapter 8: After Christmas Thoughts

Prayerful Consideration

by Shirley
Read: Matthew 28:16-20, Romans 12:1-2

Now therefore, thus says the Lord of hosts;
Consider your ways!
Haggai 1:5 (NKJV)

Each year between Christmas and New Year's Day, I take time to look back over the past year by reading through my prayer journal. I give prayerful consideration to all the things that have happened. I consider how I can better serve the Lord in the coming year and give Him thanks for His provision and protection.

Page after page of entries are filled with the names of new and long-time friends who have blessed my life in so many ways. Many of the entries mark the passing of a dear loved one from this life to everlasting life with the Lord. Sadly, other entries mark the passing of a dear loved one whom I am not certain knew the Lord as his or her Savior. Those entries always serve as an impetus to be more faithful in sharing the gospel with people. While sobering in so many ways, the entries always encourage me and remind me of the ways the Lord answered my prayers and how He provided for my every need—often before I even knew I had the need!

From time-to-time, I come across tear-stained pages with words that express my sadness, loneliness, or depression. These entries also express the cries of my heart for the Lord to give me a passion to know Him, a heart to serve Him, or eyes of love to view people.

By far, the most difficult entries for me to read are those that remind me of my grievous sins of omission and commission. They reveal my selfishness, anger, failure, and so many other sins. Yet, most of them have been marked with references to later entries that describe how the Lord forgave and restored me. There are, however, some entries with no such reference, which means I must stop to repent and ask the Lord to forgive me for that sin. And, when possible, I must go to the person whom I sinned against and ask his/her forgiveness.

Each year's prayer journal is a continuation of the story of God's redemption of and faithfulness to His people and to me. God is not faithful to us because of anything we do or have done, but because of His great mercy and love for us.

Reading through these entries also brings to mind the parable about the faithful servant and the evil servant (Luke 12:21-48). This parable ends with verse 48, "to whom much is given, from him much will be required." This verse reminds us that God will hold us accountable to use the gifts, talents, abilities, experiences, knowledge, and understanding He has given us.

Thankfully, you and I do not have to depend upon ourselves and our own strength to accomplish the things God sets before us, because as Christ-followers we can absolutely rely upon Him to equip and enable us to serve.

Take time to prayerfully consider the ministry opportunities the Lord has placed in your life, and how you can use your God-given gifts, talents, abilities, experiences, knowledge, and understanding to serve Him in the coming year.

Prayer: Heavenly Father, help us be diligent to fulfill the Great Commission, so that as we go about doing what You have called us to do, in the places You have called us to do it, that we will be disciple-makers and teach others to be disciple-makers, too. In Your precious Son's name, Amen.

Thought for the Day: Looking at the past through the lens of God's word, love, grace, mercy, and faithfulness is the only way we can make an accurate assessment.

God Takes Volunteers

by Harriet
Read: Exodus 35:4-9

Then I heard the voice of the Lord saying,
"Whom shall I send? And who will go for us?"
And I said, "Here am I. Send me!"
Isaiah 6:8 (NIV)

I have read this passage from Isaiah many times in my life. As the child of foreign missionaries, I cut my teeth on this passage. I grew up hearing that this was one of the verses God used to touch my mother's heart with the desire to become a missionary. Many times, I have heard the story of how my mom felt called to be a foreign missionary even when she was still a young girl. But, she was from a very poor and uneducated family.

She was the first person in her family to ever graduate from high school. Both of her older brothers dropped out of school after the sixth grade in order to work in the nearby textile mill and help financially support the family. Her father only had a third-grade education. He worked in the mills, like his sons and also owned a small piece of land that he farmed. He sold some of the produce and used the rest to keep his family fed. Nevertheless, my mother surrendered to God's call and went to nursing school intending to become a medical missionary. While in nursing school, she met my father—a young medical student who also felt called to foreign missions.

I have always loved my parents' story. In fact, I wrote it up in a fictionalized version in one of my books. It just makes such a good love story—she the daughter of a poor farmer and he a medical student, the son and grandson of doctors. But what makes the story so compelling is that as different as they were, they had a common calling and a shared belief that God wanted them to volunteer for His work.

God takes volunteers! Isn't that a wonderful truth? Think about it a minute. God doesn't care if a person has a lot of this earth's goods like my father's family did, or if he or she is poor like my mother's family was. God doesn't care if a person is educated or uneducated, tall or short, strong or weak. He openly receives all who volunteer for His service. He has work that can be done by anyone and everyone.

In today's reading, Moses speaks to the sons of

Israel and tells them, "This is what the LORD has commanded: From what you have, take an offering for the LORD. Everyone who is willing is to bring to the LORD an offering …." (Exodus 35:4 NIV) Everyone who is willing! Isn't that wonderful? God didn't say for the people to bring Him an offering if they were able; He said willing! God takes volunteers and gives them amazing jobs to do.

Do you remember the story of Gideon in Judges 6 and 7? How did he select his army when God told him to gather an army? Just like God, he chose those who volunteered.

It's the very beginning of a new year. Prayerfully consider what God might be asking you to volunteer for this year.

Prayer: Gracious Heavenly Father, thank You so much for using volunteers in Your work. Give us willing hearts and use us in ways we may have never imagined. In Your Son's name, Amen.

Thought for the Day: What good news it is to know that all we have to do is volunteer and God will do the rest. What might God be calling you to volunteer for this year?

The Search of the Magi

by Shirley
Read: Matthew 2:1-2, 9-12

*Where is the one who has been born
king of the Jews?
We saw His star when it rose and have
come to worship Him.
Matthew 2:2 (NIV)*

One afternoon during the Christmas season, while I was preparing to leave the house for a meeting, I could not find my keys. I searched and searched and searched. When I was about to give up and call someone to give me a ride to the meeting, I went into my office to check just one more time. I looked for the gazillionth time on the floor around the upholstered rocker where I had been sitting to review my notes for the meeting and still did not find my keys. In desperation, I pulled up the cushion of the rocker, and guess what I found?

No, I did not find my keys. I found something else—something I thought I would never see again—a ring that holds great sentimental value to me. I had lost the ring some time ago. In fact, this rocker has been moved to three different homes since I had lost the ring, and still the ring stayed securely hidden! Off-and-on for about five years, I checked and rechecked every jacket, coat, slacks, and jeans pocket, pockets in purses, boxes, drawers, crevices, and corners. Time and time again, I had looked for this ring only to be disappointed and saddened when I did not find it. I did not even look for my ring while packing to make my last move, because by then I had given up hope of ever finding it.

Finding my ring got me thinking about the Magi and their search for the King of the Jews. These men traveled a long distance to find the treasure—Jesus. What a contrast between my search for the ring and the Magi's search for the treasure! My sometimes-frantic searches often ended with me sitting on the floor crying, and that usually turned to anger at myself for being so careless, which eventually lead me to just quit looking, declaring it lost forever.

But the Magi did not get frantic or cry or get angry and give up their search because they had not yet found the treasure; they simply kept following the signs and searching. I searched for something of no lasting value; the Magi searched for the only thing that does have real, lasting value and can bring hope and eternal satisfaction.

Now, do not get me wrong, I was and am ecstatic to have found my beautiful ring. And yes, by the way, I did find my keys as well. They were still in the lock of the front door! Finding my ring and remembering all the searching I had done in vain over the past five years made me cognizant that if I am searching for anything other than Christ Himself, my searching is in vain! Psalm 107:9 (NKJV) reminds us that God "satisfies the longing soul and fills the hungry soul with goodness." How grateful I am that our search for Christ is not in vain because He draws us to Himself and enables us to find Him! Sola Gratia! (Grace Alone!)

Prayer: Lord, even as we remember the Magi's search for the Savior, may we also remember Your search for us. You came to seek and to save that which was lost. Thank You for the gift of salvation. In Jesus' name, Amen.

Thought for the Day: What are you searching for today? Are you searching for that which lasts?

Wise Men Still Seek Him

by Harriet
Read: Job 5:8-11

*Seek Him that maketh the seven stars and Orion,
and turneth the shadow of death into morning ...
the Lord is His name.*
Amos 5:8 (KJV)

"And those stars form the constellation known as Orion. You can see his belt clearly tonight."

Standing beside me, my father lifted his arm and pointed toward the clear, star-filled night sky as he spoke these words to me. My father knew every star by name. He often gazed at them through his telescope. On warm nights, he would take me outside and point to them and tell me about each one.

Some of my fondest memories of stargazing were as a child in Nigeria. Though my own father did not have a telescope on the mission field, one of my missionary uncles did. He had everything needed for a fun night of stargazing—a telescope, a knowledge of astronomy, and a little boy just my age. Our fathers had a common interest in astronomy, so many nights we accompanied them and played as we also learned from our fathers.

Those Nigerian nights stand out in my memory. There was very little electricity in that part of the world back then, which made the stars seem especially bright as they pierced the darkness with their blazing light. On cool dry nights when the dust was not too bad, the skies were filled with magical, twinkling stars! Though there could be more cloud coverage in the rainy season, it too had many clear beautiful nights.

Of all the different constellations pointed out to me in my youth, the one I can recognize most easily is Orion. My father told me the myth about Orion, how he had once been a great hunter who met his demise at the bite of a scorpion. I understood the danger of scorpions since we had them in Nigeria. The man and scorpion are outlined in that constellation, but what I recognize the most are the three stars in a row which comprise Orion's belt.

My father and missionary uncle knew about more than just the stars, they knew the maker of the stars. They were God-fearing men who served as missionaries for many years. They did not just tell my little friend and me about the stars; they told us about the God who formed the stars, too!

Like my father and uncle, the prophet Amos points us to the night sky—to Orion and other stars. Amos exhorts us to seek the one who made the stars. Job chimes in, too. Job lets us know that he sought God. Job 5:9 (NASB) says this God does "unsearchable things; wonders without number." The Magi, too, looked at the stars to understand their maker.

These are wise men: Amos, Job, the Magi, and my father and missionary uncle. Wise men seek God. They tell their children of Him and encourage others to seek Him, too. We can take the advice of these wise men and seek the wonderful God who works wonders.

Prayer: We bow our heads in awe of You, O Lord. You made the earth and the skies and all that is in them. Lord, teach us to seek You with all of our hearts. In Jesus' name, Amen.

Thought for the Day: Wise men still seek Him.

I Can't Wait for the New Year!

by Shirley
Read: Romans 8:28-30, Hebrews 10:1-4

You intended to harm me, but God intended it for
good to accomplish what is now being done,
the saving of many lives.
Genesis 50:20

There were a couple of men talking in the lobby of the Post Office one afternoon just after Christmas. I overheard the older man say, "I can't wait for the new year to get here. This has been a horrible year!"

His younger friend responded, "I can't wait either! Good riddance to this year!"

Of course, this exchange caught my attention, so I took my time walking to the mailbox, and retrieving my mail so I could hear the reasons for their sentiment. The older man talked about the prolonged illness and subsequent death of his "bride of 55 years." The younger man mentioned being laid off his job and being without work for seven months.

Later the same day, I was in the dentist office waiting for a check-up and struck up a conversation with the woman beside me. She said, "I will be so glad when this year is over!"

"Oh, why?" I replied, and she began to recount all the details of how her "former best friend" had mistreated her.

Many people share the sentiment of these three. The end of a year brings a myriad of emotions to the surface. Because of the difficulties and struggles faced throughout the previous year, many people are glad to see it end. Some have no hope that the next year will be any better, and some are hopeful that the next one will not be as difficult for them.

Many other people have had such wonderful things happen in their lives that they are sad to see the year end because they fear the good things may not continue happening. And, many more have mixed emotions, feeling simultaneously glad and sad to see the end of the year.

Throughout the years, I have found myself feeling each of these as the beginning of a new year approached. However, since I believe what God's Word says, then everything that happened in the past year, whether I perceived it as positive or negative, was for God's glory and my good. The Lord used each thing to draw me into a closer relationship with Him and to sanctify (form) me into His image.

For me, it is hard to face the fact that so much of the difficulty I encounter each year is a consequence of my own sin. Yet through the process of the Holy Spirit convicting me of my sin, I repent, ask for and receive God's forgiveness. And I learn to depend upon Him more as I realize the depth of my sin.

Do I believe what God's word says? Yes! I know it is true. So how can I do anything other than praise the Lord for the work He has done in my life during the past year? And of course, the recognition of all He has done always brings the realization of all the work that is still to be done to mold me into His image. As I pray for you, please pray that I will continue learning well the lessons presented to me during this past year and in the years to come. I thank the Lord for His love and watch-care over me throughout the years.

Prayer: Heavenly Father, give us the ability to look back on the past year and see the amazing things You have done for us. In Jesus' name, Amen.

Thought for the Day: God is at work in and through everything that happens to us.

Chapter 9: Welcome, New Year

From Rare Treasure to Junk

by Shirley
Read: Proverbs 2:1-9, Matthew 6:19-21

... lay up for yourselves treasures in heaven,
where neither moth nor rust destroys and
where thieves do not break in and steal.
Matthew 6:20 (NKJV)

On my way home from work one evening, I stopped at a store to get some gallon-sized bags to freeze the pantry stew I made the weekend before. There were still a few shelves jam-packed with Christmas items marked down for quick sale. Once Christmas was over, the items somehow morphed from rare treasures—at least that's what the pre-Christmas prices indicated—to junk, also indicated by the quick-sale prices. The aisles, that had been full of Christmas items just yesterday evening, were now filled with Valentine's and St. Patrick's Day items for sale at rare treasure prices.

I overheard one of the store clerks ask the manager if he could just shove all the Christmas junk onto one shelf to make room for the new good stuff they had. I just laughed out loud—apparently louder than I realized because the clerk asked me what was so funny.

For a split second I contemplated just smiling and walking away, and then, well, I am sure you can guess what happened. I said, "It's just humorous to me that since before Halloween all that Christmas junk had been priced at rare treasure prices. What changed? When exactly did it change from rare treasures to junk?"

The poor clerk and manager just stood there staring at me as if I were speaking some never-heard-before-language.

I knew exactly what had changed and when the items had changed from rare treasures to junk. Christmas was over, and there was no longer a demand for the Christmas items.

As I walked away, I thought about all the things with which I have done the very same thing. You know, those things that seem so important for us to get or keep that we will spend copious amounts of money and time to secure and hold onto them; only to discard, sell, or hide them away later because we found newer and better items to replace them.

We usually think the newer and better stuff will bring more comfort, satisfaction, or whatever it is that we were looking for it to fulfill. This is precisely how we are in life, isn't it? We keep searching and searching for things that will bring comfort, satisfaction, or something else, only to find they fall very short and do not fulfill the real need we have.

That is why we must seek our comfort, satisfaction, and life in and through a relationship with Jesus Christ. Only He is able to help us and give us hope. And, He will never disappoint us or fall short of our expectations.

I was also reminded that in God's eyes, His children will never be junk. Gospel singer Ethel Waters once said, "I am somebody. God don't make no junk." Each of us is unique, "fearfully and wonderfully made" as Psalm 139 expresses it. Our worth comes through our relationship with the Sovereign God of the Universe, who adopted us and made us joint heirs with His Son Jesus.

Prayer: Heavenly Father, help us carefully guard our relationship with You by spending time in the Bible and prayer, obeying Your command, and worshiping consistently with a local body of believers. In Jesus' name, Amen.

Thought for the Day: Our relationship with Jesus Christ is a rare treasure which must be cared for, nourished, and protected every moment of every day.

The Lifter of my Head

by Harriet
Read: Psalm 3:1-8

Thou O Lord are a shield to me,
my glory and the One who lifts my head.
Psalm 3:3 (NASB)

On January 13, 1984, President Ronald Reagan declared a Sunday in January to be observed in honor of the sanctity of life. Today's devotion is a retelling of a true story of a young woman named Necole who walked into a Christian crisis pregnancy center to discuss having an abortion but ended up honoring the sanctity of the life inside of her.

Necole was pregnant, alone, and scared. She was just nineteen, all alone in a big city. The grandmother who raised her lived many miles away and the father of her unborn child was dead. Facing an unwanted pregnancy with no support of any kind, abortion seemed her only option. How could she possible take care of and provide for a child by herself on what she earned? So, she entered a local crisis pregnancy center to inquire about having an abortion.

Martha worked as a counselor at the crisis

pregnancy center. What Martha noticed most about Necole was the way she kept her head down when she spoke. She only looked up occasionally during the course of the conversation. Martha spoke gently to Necole about her options, especially the possibility of giving the child up for adoption rather than aborting it. Necole listened. Necole looked small and scared and completely desperate to Martha. Yet, Martha loved her immediately. As Martha spoke, Necole, with her head still down, agreed to consider the adoption option.

Months later, after delivering a healthy baby girl, Nicole signed the adoption papers and gave her baby up to a childless couple. Her child grew up in a home with parents who loved her, and Necole moved on with her life. Through the experience, she had become like family to Martha and the other staff members of the crisis pregnancy center. In some ways, they were her only family. When she graduated from college, they attended the ceremony. Martha still has a picture of it. I saw the picture when I interviewed Martha. In it, the women from the pregnancy center are all standing beside each other encircling Necole who stood tall with head lifted high.

Through the years, Necole kept in touch with her child's adoptive parents and watched her baby grow through pictures and updates.

Some years later, Necole was diagnosed with Lupus to which she finally succumbed. In her last days, lying in a hospital bed, her strength waning, Martha and the other women from the crisis pregnancy center kept a constant vigil over her. As she lay dying, Necole confided to Martha that the proudest achievement of her life was carrying her child to term and giving her little girl the gift of life.

According to our key verse, God is the lifter of our heads. And this is the same God who creates and values the lives He has created, even the unborn ones.

Prayer: Thank You, Lord, for people like Necole who bravely carry children for others to raise. Thank You for the Marthas of the world who reach out to and offer love and support to others who are scared and alone. And thank You for being a God who lifts up our downcast heads. In Your Son's name, Amen.

Thought for the Day: What lesson is God teaching

you about the value of life? Who are you being a Martha to today? Are you reaching out and helping others like she did? Who is seeing Jesus through you?

Momentary Light Afflictions

by Harriet
Read: 2 Corinthians 4:16-18

"My yoke is easy and my burden is light."
Matthew 11:30 (NIV)

When I was about six months pregnant with
my first child, I became quite ill. One evening, my
husband took me out to eat at a nice restaurant, and
afterward I began a week-long episode of nausea
and vomiting. It started that very night when I
awoke sick to my stomach in the wee hours. I didn't
go to the doctor at first because I was in school
trying to become a registered nurse and didn't want
to miss any classes. I thought it was probably a
reaction to something I ate and would pass. And, it
was not constant. In between meals, I would be a
little better and think I could keep it down, but I
would eventually lose what I had eaten.

By the fourth day of keeping very little down,
I was daring to eat only saltine crackers and drink
sips of Sprite. I was as weak as a puppy and ended
up in the hospital with intravenous fluids. By that
time, I had not held anything down in nearly forty-
eight hours. The doctor thought it likely started
with a reaction to something I had eaten at the

restaurant, perhaps even food poisoning, but because I was pregnant, my body didn't recover like it would have if I had not been pregnant.

Somewhere around day two of the ordeal, I attended my nursing class nauseous, weak, and feeling quite poorly. My instructor could tell I was not myself and asked what was wrong. I told her of my nausea. I will always remember her response. She said, "Yes. That happens in pregnancy. It's what we refer to as one of the minor discomforts of pregnancy."

My mind screamed, "Minor?" It sure did not feel minor to me!

This little moment in my life always comes to mind when I read these verses in 2 Corinthians. In the previous chapter, in 2 Corinthians 4:8-9, the Apostle Paul says, "We are hard pressed on every side, but not crushed; perplexed but not in despair, persecuted but not abandoned; struck down but not destroyed." And yet, Paul considered these afflictions to be momentary and light.

Here we are at the beginning of a new year. Who knows what challenges may lay ahead of us before this new year becomes an old one. These verses are a good reminder for us to be strong, no matter the challenges we may be facing. Remember the attitude that Paul had? He called these afflictions momentary and light because he juxtaposed them with the eternal weight of glory that awaited him. Paul had an eternal perspective. He knew what we should know—no matter how difficult our situation is, whatever we are experiencing is just a blip on the radar screen of eternity.

Believe me, chronic nausea and vomiting for four days—enough to cause dehydration and necessitate intravenous fluids—does not feel minor! Yet, I can understand what my nursing instructor meant by the term "minor discomforts of pregnancy." A few months later, I gave birth to a beautiful, healthy baby boy, and the pain I had gone through to carry and give birth to him seemed like nothing compared to the joy of having him in my arms. My days of minor afflictions paled in comparison to the lifetime of joy he has brought me.

Prayer: Heavenly Father, Your word tells us that Your yoke is easy and Your burden is light, but we confess that sometimes it seems heavy and burdensome to us. Please help us to feel Your presence and comfort even in the most difficult of circumstances. In Your Son's name, Amen.

Thought for the Day: With Christ you can endure even the greatest of challenges.

What I Should and Could Have Done

by Shirley
Read: Philippians 3:12-16

But one thing I do: forgetting what lies behind
and straining forward to what lies ahead,
I press on toward the goal for the prize
of the upward call of God in Christ Jesus.
Philippians 3:13

I answered the phone late one New Year's Eve
and heard a voice I had not heard in over twenty-
five years. It was a friend whom I met when I lived
in the Washington, D.C., area. She had tracked me
down through several friends who live in numerous
states and cities.

I updated her on my family, and what I was
doing. When I asked her to catch me up on the past
twenty-five years of her life, she said, "Everything
was fine until this year. It's like everything came
unplugged, and it got very dark." She spent the next
hour telling me all the terrible things that happened
to her, and who was responsible for causing them
to happen. Then she said with determination in her
voice, "I will spend the rest of my life thinking
about all the things that happened this year and
figuring out what I should and could have done

differently to make things right—that way it won't seem so bad!" Hearing that absolutely broke my heart!

I am certain there are things in our past that many of us would want to go back and undo or redo. Yet, making a determined effort to spend the rest of our lives re-hashing the past in order to decide what we should or could have done differently, for the sake of making the past not seem so bad, is a miserable and colossal waste of time!

If you are living in the grip of bitterness and hurt because of things that happened to you in the past, there is hope and freedom through Jesus Christ, in whom there is rest for your soul (Matthew 11:28-29). Every moment, we as Christ-followers must choose to walk as heirs of the Sovereign God, not as slaves to anger, bitterness, and the past as the Apostle Paul wrote, "forgetting what lies behind and straining forward to what lies ahead" (Philippians 3:13-14).

Because of the finished work of Christ on the cross, instead of looking back at our past in order to rewrite our history and make it all seem better, we can view our past through the lens of God's mercy, grace, love, forgiveness, and kindness! Our sins are forgiven, our hurts are healed, and our past is redeemed. We can understand better that everything in our past has helped teach us to trust God more, and knowing that will propel us to be obedient to His commands and serve Him better now.

By God's grace, we press on into the future, untethered from the hurtful events in our past. We understand not only who we are in Christ, but also the immeasurable mercy, grace, love, forgiveness, and kindness that God generously pours out on us.

Prayer: Heavenly Father, thank You that I do not have to spend my time trying to make my past seem not so bad. Thank You that as I look at my past through the lens of Your forgiveness, love, grace, mercy, and kindness, my sins are forgiven, my hurts are healed, and my past is redeemed. Help me trust You more fully and serve You better. In Jesus' name, Amen.

Thought for the Day: Because God is rich in mercy and loves us (Ephesians 2:4-5), Christ-followers do not have to live as slaves to anger, bitterness, and the past (Philippians 3:13-14).

Always Do Your Best for Christ

by Shirley
Read: Philippians 9:24-27

*Do you not know that in a race
all the runners run,
but only one receives the prize?
So run that you may obtain it.
Philippians 9:24*

One of the highlights for missionary kids (MKs) in Nigeria, West Africa, was Mission Meeting. It was a time when the missionaries would meet to handle and discuss the business of the mission, and for the children it was time to play with some of the MKs we didn't see often because they lived in a mission station far away.

There was always a day of sports competitions—races, poll-vaulting, and a lot of other fun sports. There were two "houses" (think of two nations competing in the Olympics) that would compete against each other. Running for the Patterson House during the 1964 Mission Meeting, I won second place in the 50-yard dash for my age group. Somewhere I have the certificate to prove that I won second place! I don't remember who won first place, nor do I remember much else about the event. I know I won second place because of the certificate, a photograph with me holding the certificate, and family stories.

One thing I remember very well is that I received a loving, yet stern talking-to from my daddy because I was upset to have come in second place. Dad told me, "Sweetheart, you will not always be the best at whatever you do, however, you must always do your best!" I don't remember much else, except that my daddy scooped me up in his arms, gave me a big hug and kiss, and told me he was very proud of me.

In the 50-plus years since, my parents and other faithful Christ-followers have taught me that Christ is my only hope, and that through His Holy Spirit, He strengthens me to do everything as unto the Lord (Colossians 3:23).

Now, that doesn't mean my not-so-coveted second-place win was not important, rather it means the important thing is that I do my best for Christ—always.

I have had a myriad of opportunities to not be the best at a plethora of things, yet I stand firm in my dependence upon my Savior and Lord Jesus Christ. He took the punishment that I deserve for my sin as He was crucified, died, was buried, and then victoriously resurrected. And, He ascended to heaven where He sits at the right hand of the throne of the Sovereign God of the Universe as we read in Romans 8:34b: "Christ Jesus is the one who died— more than that, who was raised—who is at the right hand of God, who indeed is interceding for us."

Another important thing I have learned through my study and walk with Christ is that regardless of what I am facing, nothing— disappointment, fear, anger, and even elation— "will be able to separate [me] from the love of God in Christ Jesus [my] Lord" (Romans 8:38-39).

Prayer: Heavenly Father, I thank You for Your mercy, grace, and strength to always do my best for You. When things get difficult, help me look to You for strength. In Jesus' name, Amen.

Thought for the Day: Always do your best for Christ!

Chapter 10: New Beginnings

Packed Away and Hidden,
but Not Forgotten

by Shirley
Read: Isaiah 42:4-7, Luke 2:25-32

For my eyes have seen Your salvation which
You have prepared before the face of all people.
Luke 2:29-30 (NKJV)

I usually began the process of taking all the ornaments off my Christmas tree and taking down my decorations the day after Christmas. I listen to some of my favorite Christian music from the '70s and '80s during this several-day process to make certain that all the ornaments are removed from the tree, placed on tables, and grouped by type and color.

Once I finally remove all the ornaments from my Christmas tree, I begin taking the pre-lit tree apart. It has tiny white lights and some wonderful old-fashioned looking larger bulbs. Because I like colored lights on a Christmas tree, I have a lot of colored-light strands to remove. Next, I take the tree apart and pack each piece in the box. Without fail, as I am removing the pieces of the tree, I discover an ornament that I had not seen in my search to find and remove all the ornaments. It had been hidden by the green limbs, and needles, and the strands of lights.

Isn't that just like the sin that we hide so securely and deeply in our hearts? Often our sin is covered up by our arrogant blindness as well as by all the busyness of the activities and things with which we keep ourselves occupied. As the end of the year approaches, ask the Lord to peel away the things that allow you to hide sin in your heart so that you may repent of that sin. Seek forgiveness from God and ask for His strength to not continue in that sin as you put on the Lord Jesus Christ and make no provision for the flesh (Romans 13:14).

Once the tree is taken down and all the hidden ornaments are discovered, I begin to carefully wrap and pack each ornament in the appropriate box for storage until the next Christmas. As I carefully pack each ornament, I am also carefully packing and guarding the memories sparked by the ornament. These memories may include when I received or purchased the ornament, the person who gave me or made the ornament, who was with me when I found the ornament, how much Mom, Dad, or Tim loved a specific ornament, etc. Throughout the year, I may recall certain memories that the ornaments bring to mind, but many of those memories only come once a year when I actually see and touch the ornaments.

Sadly, with our Christmas ornaments and decorations, we often pack away our memories and thoughts of joy and gratitude for the arrival of Christ the Savior and the accompanying gift of salvation through Him.

This year, let's make a concerted effort to keep foremost in our minds the gift of salvation through Christ and to live our lives as representatives of the Light of the World. Let's not forget that had He not come to earth as a baby to live among us as fully God and fully man, the crucifixion and resurrection would not have been possible.

Prayer: Heavenly Father, open our blind eyes to the sin that is hidden in the dark recesses of our hearts, and keep our minds stayed on Christ, in whose name we pray, Amen.

Thought for the Day: Because Christ, the Light, dwells in us, we are to let His light shine through us.

Year-Round Nativities

by Shirley
Read: Luke 2:1-20

And she gave birth to her firstborn son
and wrapped him in swaddling cloths
and laid him in a manger,
because there was no place for them in the inn.
Luke 2:7

By now, most folks have packed away their nativities with their other decorations—but not me! I have several that I keep displayed year-round.

According to a Latin dictionary, the word nativity comes from the Latin word *nativus*, meaning "arisen by birth." A nativity scene, often just called a nativity, is a depiction of the night Jesus was born that is based on accounts found in the Bible in the books of Matthew and Luke.

The story of the first Christmas has been embellished and mixed with mythological characters so much that many people don't know what parts of the nativity and the account of Jesus' birth are biblical and which are made up. To many, Christmas bears little resemblance to the biblical accounts. Instead, Christmas has become an accumulation of imaginary fables, superstition, and pagan concepts that sound good to people because they do not know the truth of the biblical accounts.

The most important thing to realize when you look at a nativity scene is that Jesus Christ is not an imaginary, mythological, or fairy tale character— HE IS REAL! The accounts in the Bible of Jesus' birth are not imaginary tales, or superstitious beliefs, they are true accounts of actual historical events that occurred to and around real people.

As you look at things you find in nativities, go back to the Luke 2 account you read earlier and make note of which ones you find in that passage and which ones you do not. Most nativity scenes contain a stable or a cave. The Bible does not tell us exactly where Jesus was born, but we know that Mary "laid him in a manger" (Luke 2:7).

We often see the shepherds who have cattle with them and an angel above the stable. The Bible does not tell us that either were at the place Jesus was born, although they may have been. There is usually a star, we are told that there was a bright star that led the Magi to Jesus, but not to the place of His birth. Although we are not told how many Magi came, three Magi are usually depicted because of the gifts they brought: gold, frankincense, and myrrh (Matthew 2:1-11).

It is difficult to show one moment in time—the night of Jesus' birth—in one still frame. So, I keep the nativities out because they remind me of the gift God gave us—Jesus Christ His Son. This baby walked this earth as fully God and fully man, hung on the cross, died, rose from the grave, and redeemed us forever!

We do not know the exact place where Jesus was born, but we do know that he was placed in a manger and that his birth was announced to lowly shepherds. Instead of Him coming in the grandeur and pomp that usually accompanies the birth of an earthly king, He was born into humble surroundings that signaled His ministry here would be as a humble servant.

The shepherds serve as a reminder for us to tell everyone with whom we come in contact about Jesus, the Messiah!

I place all the magi in other rooms and move them closer to the nativity as Christmas nears. They never arrive at the manger, I move them so that after Christmas their journey to find Jesus begins again. Someday, I need to add a house for the wise men to bring their gifts to Jesus.

Above the shelf with the nativities is a cross. What? The cross doesn't belong with the manger … or does it? The cross reminds me that the baby in the manger grew into the man whose body was crucified on the cross. While He lived on earth, Jesus was fully God and fully man. Only a sinless man could pay the price for the sin of all mankind. It is important to remember that the finished work of Christ on the cross meant that the people of God no longer had to repeatedly offer bulls and goats (Hebrews 10) as sacrifices for their sins. On the cross redemption is perfected, and there would never need to be another sacrifice.

Prayer: Gracious Heavenly Father, thank You for the visible reminders of Your precious gift to all of us through whom we have redemption, power, and enablement to be obedient to Your teaching as we live on earth, and to live eternally with You in Heaven. In Jesus' name, Amen.

Thought for the Day: "For God so loved the world, that He gave His only Son, that whoever believes in Him should not perish but have eternal life" (John 3:16).

It's Going to Be a Good Year

by Harriet
Read: Philippians 2:14-15, Colossians 3:23

And whatever you do, whether in word or deed,
do it all in the name of the Lord Jesus,
giving thanks to God the Father through him.
Colossians 3:17 (NIV)

Our attitudes matter. We have a brand-new year ahead of us and a brand-new chance to have a good attitude about the things we will do and face this year. Our passage for today tells us to do everything without grumbling or arguing.

When my youngest son, Ty, was only in the third grade, he had an abscessed tooth. I took him to the dentist who diagnosed it, but he then referred me to an endodontist for a root canal. That took a couple of days, and by the time Ty actually had the root canal, his jaw had become sore and swollen.

The evening of his procedure, I called out for pizza to be delivered to our home for dinner because I had not had time to cook. As we sat around the table, one of Ty's older brothers asked me if we had any Ranch dressing to dip the pizza in, something he liked to do when he ate pizza. I didn't know and told him to look in the refrigerator.

Standing with his back to us and his nose in the open refrigerator, he began to fuss about the fact that, apparently, we had none. He had a mini-tirade and said something like, "Mom! We don't have any Ranch dressing! That's awful. I really wanted Ranch with my pizza. Ugh! How can anyone eat pizza without Ranch dressing!"

Ty, who loved pizza, had been trying to gingerly eat his piece. He was quite happy to finally be able to eat anything. He had not spoken much all day since his mouth had hurt to move that morning before the procedure, and it was not fully recovered yet. But provoked by his brother's tirade, he softly uttered, "And yet … somehow … life goes on."

Everyone in the room burst into laughter—my husband, daughter, and even the disappointed brother with his nose in the refrigerator.

I compare that son's sour attitude with another experience I had with my children when they were young. My husband and I have four children, but there is a gap between our first three and Ty, our youngest. This anecdote happened when the oldest three were young, long before Ty was born.

I used to fold their laundry and then have them put it away. They always grumbled and complained as they walked off to put away their laundry. One day, for no particular reason, I headed toward the laundry room and said, "Come on kids, let's have a laundry party!"

Their response was golden! Three excited children ran to the laundry room, giggling as they held their arms out for their laundry. Playing along, as I handed each his or her stack of clean laundry, I said, "Party favors for you, and you, and you!" Then I watched them skip off happily to put their laundry up. I tried it again and again. It worked every time.

Recently, I heard my now grown son ask his sister if she remembered mom's laundry parties. "Yeah," she laughed, "I always thought it was so much fun, like it really was a party. Now, of course, I realize we were just putting up laundry." They both laughed, and so did I.

So much of what we experience in life has more to do with our reactions and attitudes about things than with what really happens to us. It's the start of a new year. We can make a choice now to face the days ahead with a good attitude, as Philippians 2:14 tells us, "without grumbling or arguing."

Prayer: Gracious Heavenly Father, You are with us always. You see all we do and the attitude with which we do it. Help us to remember that whatever we are doing, we are to do it as working for You and not for people. In Your Son's name, Amen.

Thought for the Day: Somehow, life will go on. Make it a party with your attitude.

Hope—For a Few Days, or Eternity?

by Shirley
Read: Hebrews 6:13-20

*We who have fled for refuge might have strong
encouragement to hold fast to the hope
set before us.*
Hebrews 6:19

I sometimes watch sappy Christmas movies and take note of the unbiblical things I see and hear. In one movie, a supposed angel tells the spirit of a woman who is in a coma, "We've been using Christmas for a couple of thousand years to give people hope for just a couple of days."

I mentioned it to a friend who said, "Oh, they just mean for a few days they can hope against hope that things will get better." She went to the Merriam Webster site to find a definition of: "hope against hope." It means "to hope without any basis for expecting fulfillment."

I don't know about you, but having hope for just a couple of days a year is not encouraging to me. And, if there is nothing on which to base the expectation that hope will be fulfilled, is there really hope?

Now, I don't expect these movies to be gospel-centric or biblically accurate. Through years of counseling sessions, social media posts, and casual conversations, I have learned that many people I know gain their understanding of God from movies similar to this one—therein lies the problem.

At first, the words of the angel seem to make a connection between the birth of Christ and the hope of which he speaks. Yet, it is impossible to connect the birth of Christ with a hope that lasts "for just a couple of days."

What is the truth about hope? Outside of a personal relationship with Jesus Christ, there is no hope. As we read, study, memorize, and contemplate His Word in anticipation of obeying that Word, we walk in relationship with Christ. Through this relationship we come to a fuller understanding of God and who He is, and we catch a glimpse of the eternal impact His walking on this earth as fully God and fully man had in the past, is having in the present, and will have in the future for eternity. This glimpse of the eternal impact gives us hope, and not for "just a couple of days," for we are "waiting for our blessed hope, the appearing of the glory of our great God and Savior Jesus Christ" (Titus 2:15).

Charles Wesley wrote the words of "Come Thou Long Expected Jesus" reminding us that Jesus is the "hope of all the earth" (Psalm 65). J. Wilbur Chapman wrote the words of "One Day" that say Jesus is the "hope of the hopeless, my Savior is He!" (If you don't know these hymns, look them up online, and you will be blessed.)

Paul David Tripp said, "You have one place of hope, security and rest. It is found in these words— 'God is love.'"

As Christ-followers, we are reconciled to God by the death of Jesus so that we are presented to God as holy and blameless before Him (Colossians 1:22). The next verse here tells us how to grasp hold of the hope for which we have been talking. "If indeed you continue in the faith, stable and steadfast, not shifting from the hope of the gospel that you heard, which has been proclaimed in all creation under heaven ...." (Colossians 1:23).

Praise God that our hope is firmly placed in Him—not for just a few days—but for eternity. Soli Deo Gloria (To the glory of God alone)!

Prayer: Heavenly Father, thank You that our hope is based upon You alone, and therefore is not in vain. Help us learn to know and trust You more. In Your Son's name, Amen.

Thought for the Day: Because God is love, we find security and rest as we hope in Him.

New Year … Same God

by Harriet
Read: Hebrews 13:5-8

*Jesus Christ is the same yesterday
and today and forever.
Hebrews 13:8 (NASB)*

As I drove past a neighborhood church sometime last January on my way to take my son to school, I could not help but notice the sign in the front of the church. This large sign near the road often has comments that catch my attention, and that January day was no exception. "New Year … same gracious God" were the words written for all passersby to see.

"New Year … same gracious God." The words struck me and continued to roll around in my head all day.

"What a comfort!" I thought.

Driving on toward my son's school, that thought took root in my heart. We live in such a fast-paced world. Things change all around us all the time. They change every day in every area of our lives. We face new breakthroughs in science, new gadgets to possess, new occurrences around the world, and new technologies to learn. Just as we think we have mastered the computer, there are iPhones, iPads, Blackberries, Kindles, and all sorts of other things to figure out. There are things in existence today that we could have never even dreamed of just a few years ago. If we miss out on reading the paper or watching the news for a few days, sometimes we are shocked at the changes we learn.

My children have words in their vocabulary that I had never heard of when I was young. When I was a child, a mouse was a small rodent that one tried to avoid. Today, though a mouse is still that small rodent, it is also an important piece to your computer. And a pad—now that is an evolving word if ever there was one! To my parents a pad was either a cushion or a small tablet of paper on which to write. To my generation it was also a person's apartment. I remember the hip sounding phrase, "Hey baby, do you want to come over to my pad?" Of course, what was hip then sounds weird now. And today, a pad is a place on which your mouse rests (your computer mouse that is).

My youngest son understands new technologies that I do not even know exist. I remember learning to type on a typewriter, something he thinks went into extinction about a hundred years ago. In fact, I am a constant source of entertainment to him with all the things I do not seem to know. He tells me I am old. But even my older children do not know some of the things he knows. The world of technology has changed that rapidly.

Amid all of the rapid change, isn't it nice to know that the Lord never changes? Hebrews 13:8 tells us that "He is the same yesterday, and today, and tomorrow, and forever!" This truth is also stated in other parts of the Bible. Malachi 3:6 says plainly, "I the Lord do not change." I am so thankful for this truth!

Prayer: Father in Heaven, we are so grateful that You are who You are. You have been the same since the beginning of time, and we know You can be trusted with our changing tomorrows. In Your Son's name, Amen

Thought for the Day: We may be facing a new year, but we are facing it with the same God who saw us through the previous one!

From Africa to America, Lifelong Friends

March 14, many years ago ...

Deep in the heart of the African jungle in the Niger River Delta of eastern Nigeria, the first cry of a newborn baby echoed from a small jungle hospital. The baby was a girl, the third child of medical missionaries, Alice and Keith Edwards.

"We'll name her Harriet Clarice after both of her grandmothers." Alice smiled as she spoke; peering at the tiny squirmy ball of flesh she had just given birth to with the help of her husband and a missionary friend, Jo Scaggs. Being the only doctor for miles around, Keith delivered his own child on that early March morning. Jo, a missionary nurse helped, of course. They were the only three missionaries stationed at this remote jungle hospital in the village of Joinkrama, Nigeria—Alice, Keith, and Jo Scaggs. Though this was Jo's permanent station, Alice and Keith were only there for one year to relieve another missionary doctor and his family who were in the States on furlough.

Joinkrama is located across the Niger River in the far eastern part of Nigeria. There were no bridges when Alice and Keith set out for their new home so long ago. They crossed the river in a large passenger thatched-roof, canoe-type boat. Joinkrama lies in the small section of Nigeria that is within the tropical rain forest. And it fit the role, with monkeys swinging happily in the trees, parrots, canaries, and other colorful birds sitting on branches and thatched roofs of the houses, and elephants in the nearby jungle sometimes getting a little too close for comfort. And of course, there were poisonous snakes to watch out for and crocodiles in the river. Children never played on the riverbanks, and swimming was absolutely prohibited! It was in this almost magical setting that Harriet was born.

Though the little jungle hospital was equipped for surgery, and the preferred place to give birth, it was not where Alice wanted to convalesce after giving birth. She wanted to be home in their mission-built house with her other children playing nearby.

Alice was transported home on a stretcher carried by four men, as it was much too far to walk just after giving birth. As Alice lay on the stretcher with newborn Harriet sleeping in her arms, the villagers they passed feared the worst. Thinking she and the baby had died in childbirth, people began to weep and mourn.

"Ma, you must sit up. The people think you have died!" the men carrying Alice told her, once they realized why the people were crying.

Alice sat up and waved. She also held baby Harriet up for them to see. The villagers' weeping turned to dancing and cheering. They formed a celebratory throng behind the stretcher and accompanied her home, dancing, and praising God the entire way.

Harriet and her family stayed in this remote part of Nigeria for a year until the other family returned from furlough. At that time, they went for another year to Oyo, Nigeria, to language school and then on to Ogbomoso in central Nigeria, where they stayed the next ten years. Keith practiced medicine at the hospital in Ogbomoso, and Alice worked with him as a nurse.

October 24 of the same year ...

Deep in the Yoruba country of southwestern Nigeria, some 260 miles away from Joinkrama, piercing through the tropical night sounds, was heard the first cry of another baby born in a guesthouse in Ogbomoso, under the shade of a mango tree. This baby was also a girl, the fourth child of missionaries Jeannie and Ray Crowder.

Early in the morning, missionary doctors Bill Williams and Ruth Berry, the second woman to ever graduate from the Medical College of Alabama, delivered this baby girl. Single missionary nurse, Lolete Dotson, an MK from South Africa who served a total of 25 years in

Nigeria, stood beside the baby's mom, holding her hand, wiping her face with a wet cloth, and whispering encouraging words.

The family thought the fourth baby would be a second Timothy, yet Shirley Jeanne arrived instead. Ray always said he named her for actress Shirley Temple whom he claimed was his childhood sweetheart. The Nigerians gave her the name Bamidele, which means "come home with me." It is a name given to a child born in a place that is not his or her parent's home. The name was given by the Nigerians to missionary babies, both male and female, who were born there. This is Harriet's Nigerian name as well.

Missionaries built the Baptist guesthouse where this baby was born so that traveling missionaries and visitors to Ogbomosho could have a place to stay. It was named Frances Jones in memory of a missionary to Nigeria who died of yellow fever many years earlier. This was the temporary home for big brothers Paul and Tim, six years old and twenty-two months old, respectively. They escorted their mom to Ogbomoso to await the arrival of their new brother or sister, since there were no medical professionals in the predominantly Muslim northern city of Keffi where the Crowders served.

Shirley's father, Ray, was in Kaduna auditing books. He gave oversight to and helped build a hospital and ministered at the pastor's school there. Ten-year-old big sister, Anne, was attending the school for MKs, Newton Memorial in Osogbo, 40 miles away from Ogbomoso. A missionary in

Ogbomoso called the school, and one of the missionary aunts gave Anne the news that she now had a baby sister. Anne's MK suitemates, Sheryl and Charlotte, were with her when she heard the news and were quick to claim Shirley as their baby sister, too! It would be a couple of weeks before anyone could drive Anne from Osogbo to Ogbomoso to meet her new baby sister.

Several years later, the Crowders moved to Ogbomoso. Ray served as administrator of the 96-bed hospital, and Jeannie taught kindergarten and ministered to the Nigerian women with home visits and Bible studies. Harriet's parents worked at the Ogbomoso hospital with Ray.

Shirley and Harriet as children.
Shirley is the blonde girl in plaid kneeling,
and Harriet is standing just
behind and to the side of Shirley,
next to a tall boy.

Lifelong Friends

Harriet ended up living just up the dirt road from Shirley. They played together nearly every day and formed a friendship that remained, even after years and distance separated them. Today, Harriet is a wife of more than 39 years, a mother of four, and a grandmother of two. She is a multi-published author and freelance writer. Along with her numerous books, her work has appeared in publications by Lifeway, Focus on the Family, David C. Cook, Standard Publishing, and more.

Shirley is passionate about disciple-making, which is conducted in and through a myriad of ministry opportunities that include writing, biblical counseling, teaching Bible studies, and speaking at women's conferences.

She is a biblical counselor and co-host of "Think on These Things," a Birmingham, Alabama, radio/TV program for women. Shirley is commissioned by and serves on the national advisory team for The Addiction Connection.

Several of her articles have appeared in "Paper Pulpit" in the Faith section of *The Gadsden Times*. She is also a writer for David C. Cook, Student Life, and Woman's Missionary Union publications. She is published as an author, co-author, and contributing author.

Shirley has spiritual children and grandchildren serving the Lord in various ministry and secular positions throughout the world.

Follow the Authors

Shirley Crowder
Blog: www.ThroughtheLensofScripture.com
Facebook: /shirleycrowder
Twitter: @ShirleyJCrowder
Amazon: amazon.com/author/shirleycrowder

Harriet E. Michael
Blog: www.harrietemichael.blogspot.com
Facebook: /harrietmichaelauthor
Amazon: amazon.com/author/harrietemichael

About the Illustrator

Kristin Michael

Kristin is a freelance artist whose preferred medium is oil painting. Her style is contemporary expressionist with a focus on light and water. She obtained her liberal arts degree at Bellarmine University in Louisville, Kentucky, with a double minor in fine arts and literature.

Kristin continued her education at St. Catherine College in Bardstown, Kentucky, where she earned an associate degree in Cardiac Sonography.

She is now employed full-time by Kentucky Children's Hospital as a pediatric and adult congenital cardiac sonographer (she performs ultrasounds on children and adults with congenital heart disease).

Kristin works hard in her healthcare and artistic endeavors as a single mother in order to take care of her sweet young son who is the light of her life. You can find more of Kristin's artwork at **www.instagram.com/kiki_paintings**.

Also by the Authors
Prayer Project

Glimpses of Prayer
by: Shirley Crowder & Harriet E. Michael

We have two primary means of communicating with God—the Bible and prayer. But what is prayer, really? This book of 50 devotions will help you look at many facets of prayer. Each devotion is centered around prayer and focuses on verses from the Old Testament and the New Testament that speak about prayer. We pray the Holy Spirit would work through these devotions to help you gain a better understanding of prayer, and to ignite or deepen your passion to know Him better, resulting in you experiencing a richer more powerful prayer life.

Available on Kindle and in paperback from Amazon and most bookstores by request.

Prayer: It's Not About You
by: Harriet E. Michael

Is prayer a mighty spiritual weapon or a waste of time? Is it something to be engaged in fiercely, as if wielding a weapon in the midst of a spiritual battle, or is it just a personal practice to achieve a calmer, more focused and disciplined life? Does prayer really change anything?

Those questions and so many more are discussed inside the pages of this book. The book does not simply offer one writer's perspective on the topic of prayer. Instead, it delves deep into Scripture to see how prayer is presented in God's Word.

The book offers a thorough study of prayer from a biblical perspective. Moving from Genesis to Revelation, this book looks at instances of prayer as recorded in the Bible, exploring the who, what, where, when, how, and why.

Available on Kindle and in paperback from Amazon and most bookstores by request.

Study Guide on Prayer—A Companion to Prayer: It's Not About You
by: Shirley Crowder

This study guide is designed to help you study, individually or in a group setting, the book, ***Prayer: It's Not About You***. As you work your way through this study guide, you will read the book chapter by chapter. Then you will be guided to interact with the teachings, principles, and practices contained in Scripture and ***Prayer: It's Not About You***.

It is the author's prayer that as you work through this study guide, you will gain knowledge and understanding. Through the work of the Holy Spirit, you will incorporate the teachings, principles, and practices in the book into your prayer life so that as your passion to pray increases, it will result in a strengthened relationship with God the Father, through Jesus Christ His Son.

Available on Kindle and in paperback from Amazon and most bookstores by request.

Coming Soon!
Prayer Warrior Confessions
November 2018

Written by a Bolivian missionary, both of these collections of devotions offer encouragement and hope for the woman feeling pressed on all sides.

Scripture References

Old Testament

Genesis 3:15	p. 126	Psalm 37:23-26	p. 51
Genesis 50:20	p. 167	Psalm 65	p. 205
Exodus 35:4	p. 160	Psalm 74:13-17	p. 69
Exodus 35:4-9	p. 158	Psalm 74:16-17	p. 69
Deuteronomy 6:5	p. 85	Psalm 96:1-3	p. 114
Deuteronomy 16:14	p. 145	Psalm 98:1-6	p. 114
Judges 6	p. 160	Psalm 98:4	p. 116
Judges 7	p. 160	Psalm 100	p. 74
1 Samuel 14:6	p. 38	Psalm 100:4	p. 74
1 Kings 19:11-13	p. 101	Psalm 107:9	p. 163
1 Kings 19:12	p. 101	Psalm 110:1	p. 127
1 Chronicles 16:33	p. 17	Psalm 139	p. 174
1 Chronicles 16:34	p. 26	Psalm 145:4-7	p. 138
Job 5:8-11	p. 164	Psalm 147:3	p. 29
Job 5:9	p. 166	Psalm 148	p. 16
Psalm 2:7	p. 126	Psalm 148:3-6	p. 16
Psalm 3:1-8	p. 176	Proverbs 2:1-9	p. 172
Psalm 3:3	p. 176	Proverbs 25:11	p. 20
Psalm 7:17	p. 114	Ecclesiastes 3:11-13	p. 105
Psalm 17:6-8	p. 56	Isaiah 6:1	p. 53
Psalm 17:8	p. 56	Isaiah 6:8	p. 38 & 158
Psalm 19:14	p. 20 & 24	Isaiah 6:9	p. 126
Psalm 22:1	p. 126	Isaiah 7:14	p. 126
Psalm 24:7-10	p. 134	Isaiah 9:6	p. 134
Psalm 24:9	p. 135	Isaiah 11:1-6	p. 122
Psalm 27:4	p. 59	Isaiah 30:15	p. 14
Psalm 33:3	p. 85	Isaiah 42:4-7	p. 192
Psalm 34:7-9	p. 81	Isaiah 53:3-12	p. 127
Psalm 34:8	p. 81 & 82	Isaiah 55:12	p. 17
Psalm 34:9	p. 82	Isaiah 61:1-3	p. 29
Psalm 34:10	p. 82	Amos 5:8	p. 164
Psalm 34:11	p. 83	Micah 5:2	p. 126
Psalm 34:13	p. 83	Zechariah 9:9	p. 127
Psalm 34:14	p. 83	Haggai 1:5	p. 154
Psalm 37:23	p. 51	Malachi 3:6	p. 209

New Testament

Hymn Index

**Thank you
for reading our books!**

**Look for other books
published by**

Pix-N-Pens Publishing
An imprint of Write Integrity Press
www.WriteIntegrity.com

Made in the USA
Middletown, DE
29 November 2018